5.6.13

Tim,

   May this help you
and your region
further down the
Journey of success!

            Be wonderful

1

The Journey

The Evolution of a Financial Advisor

Ken Doyle

Founder of

Getting Results Coaching

7290 B. Investment Drive
Charleston, SC 29418
USA

Doyle, Ken

The Journey, The Evolution of A Financial Advisor

ISBN-13: 978-1456474706

Printed and bound in the United States of America

Contents

The Journey

The Evolution of a Financial Advisor

"You are the sun and whatever you shall shine upon shall grow"

Chapter 1

Attention is best

A big man, his head slightly down and his body propelling forward as if caught between a skip and a fall, barreled from the door of the Landmark Tavern. His gray trench coat, thrown open by the cold November wind of the city, revealed a finely tailored suit covering ample shoulders as well as an ample belly. The burdens of life were etched in the lines of his forehead. His body and demeanor was that of a football player who continued to eat as if he was to play a game on Saturday, but who has long since retired, somewhat reluctantly, to the business world.

Adam Arbor had stopped in for one drink, but stayed for more. Ordinarily a loving man, he had still had his share of frustrations, and his boss, Herb Faye, had dragged him over the coals that morning over his sales. The drubbing seemed to be just one more thing, and he found that the tavern suited his needs that afternoon. Anchored on the corner of Hamm and Center streets in the dilapidated historic district, it was a place that attracted a clientele from the rough as well as upscale parts of town. Built with bricks made from the mud of the swamp that the city was raised, the tavern had a large bay window with a view of the crossroads. The floor was aged oak, stained and worn, and vintage layers of dust enveloped the top-shelf liquor bottles that were largely untouched by customers who drank to forget, to get a respite, or to medicate. It was a place time seemed to have forgotten; few people cared about the rumor that the founding fathers had plotted revolution in its quiet corners, away from their colonial masters.

Leaving the tavern, the big man rolled down the steps toward a business appointment over bills he wasn't quite sure why he had. He didn't want this meeting, and he felt guilty about needing to dull the edge of the day. Worse still, the Jack Daniels he just consumed had exactly the opposite effect.

Heading into the bar for his weekly pint was an older, well-dressed gentleman, perhaps in his early fifties, moving with the unhurried grace of a lifelong athlete and the confidence of a self-made man. Bounding up the stairs, he saw the big man hurtling towards him, oblivious to his surroundings.

"Attention is best," the man with gray hair softly commanded, as he molded his body to avoid the descending water buffalo.

"What," the big man mumbled, his mind swimming.

"Attention is best," the older man repeated, in a commanding voice that echoed with genuine caring.

Arbor tilted his head and stared down, his entire bulk expanding into his chest. His mind exploded, filled with the drunken clarity of anger. 'No one commands Adam Arbor! How dare he speak to me in that tone,' he thought. 'Doesn't he know who I am?'

The gray-haired gentleman could read his reaction, and with a slight shrug of his shoulders he calmly said for a third time,

"Attention is best. That's all I said."

"Is that what you said?" hissed Adam. "What the hell do you mean by that?" Adam Arbor thought he had control of his temper but there was something about the man in front of him that clouded his mind, much like a red cape waved in front of a bull.

The older man was one who might have commanded respect from others, but Adam had come to expect deference, and to believe he deserved it. That had been challenged earlier in the day, his lousy boss grinding him about his sales, and with his mind polluted by whiskey and what felt like the flotsam of his life, he was in no mood to deal with this little puissant.

"All I said is that attention is best. And if you would please step aside I have an appointment at the bar." The gray-haired man stepped forward, as if expecting to be allowed to pass, but Adam did not move.

"You can't talk to me like that," Adam snarled, with the threat of goring this man, lancing each word.

"No? Unfortunately I already have. With proper inquiry you will see that attention is best. Now please allow the liquor to stop making a puppet of you and let me pass." The gray-haired man spoke as if he was a fifth-grade teacher speaking to one of his unruly students. The statement was not meant to demean, simply to remind the student to get back to the assignment. There was no question of authority; the older man was secure in his position, no matter Arbor's reaction.

Adam's mind was racing to find a time when someone had not heeded his size, bulk and presence. He couldn't understand how this old man was acting, as if Arbor was nearly invisible, a small boy who had never touched a weight in his life.

It was infuriating, for if there was anything that Adam demanded from others it was respect. He wasn't always sure why he de-served it but it was something he had gotten all of his life. On better days, he linked it vaguely to his having played at Texas in college, a success he had carried into his career, but this was not the best of days, and the old man displayed no deference, no respect.

There was another thing about the man; it was his seemingly total lack of intimidation by Adam. Most people backed down when they saw the size and scope of Adam Arbor. This guy was acting as if he had absolutely nothing to worry about from the presence of Adam, as if he was free of fear. Clouded recognition of this agitated Adam. 'How can my bulk not matter to this guy?' he wondered.

There was a moment's pause before his mood translated into action. Adam did not know what it was that ignited his fury. Perhaps something in the man's bearing or his words, or maybe it was a volatile combination of his earlier meeting with Faye, Jack Daniels and his miserable experience of life, but he let fly.

Chapter 2

Reality shifts

The smaller man's reaction was swift and overwhelming. Surprised, Adam felt a paroxysm of pain, thinking to himself, 'Oh my God!' His wrist throbbed, as if the bones had splintered, and he could feel fingers burrowing into his throat. The man's grip expertly pushed aside muscle to expose the jugular, the fingers mining into the source of Adam's life. The urge to succumb rose in Adam's mind, as he thought with regret of things still unaccomplished.

'What of my boys?' Thoughts continued to erupt in his mind, 'What have I done to deserve this? My wife...does she know that I love her? When was the last time I told her? My last words to her were a grunt because I was annoyed that we were out of milk.' Even as his breath was choked off and his vision blurred from tears, he was struck by the mundane details that took on meaning.

With pain in every part of his body, sadness washed in. As Adam's body was deprived of oxygen, he went slack, collapsing backward against the stairs. His thoughts raced, but he was unable to say anything; he could only stare upward into his opponent's eyes. 'I'm not mad at you! Can't you understand? I was only trying to scare you! Most people simply run away from me. You see, I played football in college. I have lifted weights most of my life. I am a big man. You were supposed to run away!'

The old man simply stared, his eyes, piercing blue, seeming to dig into Adam's head. Looking at him. 'Oh man, this is not right' thought Adam. 'I want to live. I want to make up for all the wrong I have done.' Shaking as the man's grip slowly tightened, Adam knew that he should be able to struggle. He was bigger, stronger, and younger, but there was so much pain.

He could feel himself slipping away when the tears being choked from his eyes were replaced by genuine tears, his mouth curling as he choked out sobs. Squinting, Adam saw in the other man's eyes not hate, but compassion. 'Is he speaking to me?'

The Old Man's voice was serene considering the pain he was causing: "Is what's gnawing at you worth your life?" And he let go.

'I can breathe!' Adam collapsed entirely, his nose and eyes running and the world a haze obscured by sadness and nausea.

'This man, how did he do it? He looks like he is 50. I am only 38. I'm taller, I outweigh him. This is just wrong. How did he put me in so much pain and make me utterly helpless?'

"You could have killed me," he gasped. "How did you do that? No one has ever man-handled me before. You didn't even seem to make an effort. Who are you?"

The older man looked down into Adam's eyes as the big man wiped his nose on the sleeve of his suit. He seemed peaceful, serene, even blissful. A moment after what he thought would be his death, Adam now felt safe. But not secure, as he thought about the failure of his strength, the lack of effect that his size had had on his opponent. 'Without that, who am I now?'

The other man seemed to know Adam's thoughts, but said, with a wink and a warm smile, "Perhaps you will take heed of what I said and then again perhaps you won't. But you should know this, before I go and get the cocktail that you nearly interfered with:

Don't be under the illusion that I was here accidentally." With that he bounded up the stairs and into the tavern. As the pain ebbed, the fog of whiskey returned, less potent than before but still befuddling. Adam remained on the stairs, sagging back in a slump. 'How the hell did this happen? Take heed of what I said... what the hell did he say? Attention is best. What does that mean?'

A few minutes later, and no clearer in his thoughts, Adam struggled to his feet, trying to collect himself and straighten his disheveled suit. He needed to see his wife, but first was that damn appointment.

Chapter 3

The Meeting with Biggus

Adam turned his head back to look at the door of the Landmark Tavern and stared at it like a man who crawls away from a head-on collision to look back at his crumpled vehicle and realizes he is unscratched. If someone had been looking at him they would have seen a man trying to process the improbable as if he just saw a cow fly or an angel descend from heaven.

'Damn,' Adam thought to himself, 'I need to get to that meeting.' With that thought he rearranged his suit the best he could, brushed the dirt off his knees and shuffled in the direction of Mr. Biggus's office.

As Adam walked towards his appointment he had a surreal sense of the city. Passing the storefronts and apartment houses, it was as if he was watching a movie instead of living his life. He felt as if he was an alien in his own body, that the encounter of a few moments before somehow shifted his sense of who he was, and he did not understand. Things did not seem as they were just a few hours ago. Everything changed and Adam did not understand why. He still felt intoxicated, but the run-in with death had knocked his alcohol buzz clear from his system. It was more like the fabric of reality had been torn asunder, and it scared him. What he had always believed to be true had been proven false. Adam felt the way a man feels when he receives divorce papers unexpectedly, or a loyal company man gets downsized or an adult child discovers they were adopted, but he did not have time to process. He needed to get to his appoint-ment with Mr. Biggus.

Adam turned the corner and saw the sign for Richard Biggus and Associates and bile rose into his throat. Biggus was one of his earliest clients, one that he'd cold-called and convinced to buy bonds. He remembered he really had to work to get this guy's business and he would only buy if he had the lowest price, but with Adam's consistency Biggus over time had become one of his largest clients. Biggus knew that and took advantage of it. He always demanded price breaks or prime tickets to sporting or civic events. Adam remembered a recent call when Biggus wanted 2 tickets to a local play that was sold out.

"Arbor, get me two tickets or I am pulling the account," he'd said, "and make sure neither you or any of your associates are anywhere near me – I don't want to meet you there, not before or after the event. I don't need to develop any more friends. And I want those tickets by tomorrow."

Adam remembered with disgust that he'd spent the entire day securing those tickets at the cost of about a grand, not to mention the lost work time. Although Adam made a lot of money from Biggus he always dreaded interacting with him, especially in person. The phone was bad enough but when you had to look at his scowl it made Adam wonder why he had not become a dentist.

Adam faced the door of Biggus and Associates, still somewhat detached from reality, and walked in.

Biggus looked up from his desk. "You're late." Seeing Adam's disheveled clothes, he said with a sneer "you look horrible – like some one just kicked your ass! I am sure you deserved it!" He let out a derisive laugh and shook his head." I don't know why I keep you as my advisor!" Biggus snapped.

"Sorry. I had a bit of a run-in you would never believe."

"Don't care, Arbor, I'm a very busy and important man and my money is very important to me! Why can't you pick the same great stocks that my Merrill guy does? He always has great ideas that work? But you? It seems I give you all the ideas Arbor!" Biggus was in fine form, his words a staccato rhythm spat from a machine gun mouth.

Adam was being assaulted by a whirlwind of accusations, he wanted to reply but he knew better. Adam always gave Biggus ideas and the ones that worked Biggus would claim as his own, and then the crazy pork belly stuff Biggus would come up with and execute, he would blame their failure on Adam. Adam also knew he made a ton of money from Biggus, and money was all that mattered, he thought.

"How was that play I sent you to?" Adam lofted a serve to change the nature of the conversation.

"Horrible, stupidest thing I ever saw, how could you get me tickets to such a lousy piece of crap?"

"How could I?" Adam stammered. "You asked me to get them for you."

Watching Biggus' lips distracted Adam, triggering him to remember a voice saying 'Do not think I was here accidentally' and there were the blue eyes and the brush with death again.

"Why are you here Arbor?" foamed Biggus.

'Yea,' Adam thought, 'why am I here? Is what I am doing a worthy way to live my life? I almost died 20 minutes ago. Is this really how I want to live my life?'

"Yes." Now Adam was muttering. "Why am I here? Who Am I? Why am I alive?"

"What are you muttering about Arbor?" sneered Biggus.

"Nothing, you wanted to meet me?"

"Yes that is right. Do you value my business, Arbor?"

"Yes, of course I do."

"Well if you would like me to keep my business with you I need you to rebate back to me half of all your fees."

"What? I can't do that. It's illegal."

"What is illegal is for you to suck away my money through management and 12b1 fees. I want my money back. I should just manage the money myself, and I will if you do not discount your rates."

"Look, I told you, it's illegal."

"I don't care. Just bring me an envelope each month with the cash after you get your commission check from the office."

Adam was dazed. He wondered how this could be happening to him. He gave Richard outstanding service, was always there, at beck and call, and now he wanted a rebate and dropping off envelopes each month? Not only this but his size fails him and a simple phrase continues to echo in his head, 'attention is best.'

"Make your own call Arbor. If I don't get my envelope from you, I am pulling all of my money from your candy ass firm. And don't think you can tell anyone about this. I will totally deny it and still pull all my money from your firm. So you need to decide, is half better than zero? And before you go, give me $100 bucks so I can take my wife out for dinner to make up for that lousy play."

Adam dug into his wallet, handed him a hundred, and left the building with his mind whirling a symphony of questions: What is going on with my life? What have I done to deserve this? Who am I? What am I doing with my life?

His wandering continued until he made it home.

Chapter 4

The hangover

"Honey, are you all right? Oh my God, what's happened to you?" Evelyn gasped.

Adam stood before her, disheveled, his shoulders hunched forward and his head down, his suit a shell encasing him, looking as if he had just survived an earthquake or, more ominously, that something precious had just been lost forever. 'He looks so small,' she thought to herself, 'not the big man I married.'

Evelyn and Adam had been married for ten years, mostly a good marriage. She loved him, but things had changed so much in the last few years. Evelyn had seen Adam draw away, keeping to himself, retreating into himself. He had stopped communicating with her in the way he used to. Somehow a gap had been created between them, a gap that sometimes felt more like an ocean.

Eve's voice slipped with concern, "Honey, what happened?"

"You would never believe this day Eve." Adam's hollowed eyes gazed at Eve as his meaty hands covered his face with lips trembling. His big hands could not hold back the torrent of emotion: "I was almost killed today Evelyn! Some guy says, 'attention is best' and before I know it his hand was around my throat and it felt like he was going to rip off my arm!"

"What?" Eve gaped. "Are you okay Adam? Let me see." She loosened his tie and unbuttoned the top button of his collar to expose his neck gasping at the sight of five separate welts around his Adam's Apple. "Oh my god! Did you get attacked by a gang? Where the hell were you?"

"I was at the Landmark Tavern," Adam replied sheepishly.

"What were you doing in that part of town? Jesus, Adam, are you having an affair? Did someone's husband and a bunch of his friends jump you? My god it must have been something bad. Who in their right mind would go after a person as big as you?" Eve crossed her arms and stared vehemently at him, her anger rising as a defensive screen came up in her mind.

Adam looked at her, and everything spilled forth. "Evelyn, I am not having an affair. You should know better than that. I was at the tavern because Herb ripped in to me today." He let out an exasperated sigh. "I'm sick of what I do for work and sick of all the crap I have to deal with. I had an appointment tonight with a client I really dislike so I figured I would go down to the tavern to take the edge off. I had a few Jack and Cokes. While I was there, I guess I got to thinking about how much my business sucks and how much my life seems to have stalled."

Adam looked directly at Eve. "You know when we first got married everything seemed possible and our lives were exciting. My job was exciting. Now, my job sucks," Adam corrected himself, "I hate what I do but we needed it to survive back then. My job was a driving force for us to live the life we thought we wanted, to keep the bill collectors off our backs, to keep food on the table, to buy this house. So I was willing to do anything for anybody in order to build my business so we could survive. Well Evelyn, we have survived. But today so much flashed before me. Today I began to question everything."

"So how did you get those bruises on your neck?" Eve inquired.

"As I said, Herb was lighting in to me today," Adam lied.

Herb Fay was Adam's boss, the manager at Talbot Hill Securities. Adam had been at Talbot for 10 years now, as long as he had been married to Evelyn. To everyone on the outside he had a very successful career – lots of clients, selling lots of stuff and the third largest producer in the office for five years in a row. He'd made the same amount of money for the last five years but he seemed to be working more and enjoying it less. He dreaded each day he went to the office, but the money was coming in.

"Herb said that I need to improve my numbers. He said that I have been running in neutral for a long time. He kept singing activity drives production. He said I needed to run more direct mail campaigns and start smiling and dialing for dollars. He called me a slacker, says I don't work hard enough, despite the fact that I'm in the office at 7 a.m. and don't go home until 7 p.m. every day. I hardly see the boys anymore. I am freaking busy all day and then that Ascot-wearing nut case tells me that I'm not working hard enough! He says that I have to put my nose to the grindstone and grind it out. What the hell am I supposed to do?" Adam's frustration was visible in the lines of his face and his monologue continued. "This was a day baby, not only was Herb chewing me out but I must have had every client call me with some sort of fire! All I heard today was, 'how could you do this to my account?,' 'why haven't you called me lately?' 'Where is my dividend check?' 'Why did you invest in bonds when we should've put the money in stocks?' 'Why did we put money in stocks when we should have invested in bonds?' 'I need my money now!' All day this is what I heard, whine, whine, whine I need this, I need that, why did you do this, why did you do that. It was enough to drive me nuts. My phone would not stop ringing, and the damn e-mail box was always full. It was ridiculously busy today, and totally unproductive."

"Then listen to this, hon, Mr. Biggus calls and says he needs to meet me tonight to discuss his portfolio. He does not ask, he demands. He calls and shouts, 'Arbor, you'll see me tonight or I'm pulling all of my money out from under your miserable firm. You hear me? I'm tired of all you idiots screwing up my finances. I can't believe what an ass I am to put my money with you buffoons!'" Adam grunted out a derisive snort. "Not a good day. So I left the office a little early to prepare for my meeting with Mr. Biggus." Looking at his wife, he continued. "Yeah I know, prepping in a bar is not the best way to get ready for a meeting. But this guy is such an ornery old prick. I needed something to dull the sting of his words and clear his cloud of condescending air."

"So what happened baby?" asked Eve. Her voice had changed from defensive to compassionate.

He shook his head, his eyes shifting as he searched for an explanation. "Eve it happened so fast, I honestly don't know. All I remember is I am leaving the bar, not very happy about my obligation to go and see Mr. Biggus. I know as soon as I see him all he is going to say is how lousy I am.

Sometimes I wonder why I even deal with this guy. I guess it's because I am a whore. I need the money he gives us. It's lots of money so I've got to do what he commands." Adam recalled the experience with a distant look in his eyes. "So I bang through the doors getting ready to go to the car and this old guy is walking in. Before I get a chance to move, I guess it was Mr. Jack Daniels slowing me down, we almost collide. I thought I was going to full bore barrel over him." Eve watched her husband with intent.

"You know Eve, I still can't believe it. He was like smoke. He moved and curled his body so I did not touch him. I was convinced that we would both fall down the stairs. But he just molded around me and then he said, "Attention is best."

"He said, attention is best?" repeated Eve.

"Can you believe that f'ing prick!"

"And then he attacked you?" asked Eve incredulously.

"Well no," Adam stated as he stared sheepishly at the design of their rug.

"What did he look like so we can get a description to the police?"

"Well he had gray hair, probably around 50 years old with very sharp blue eyes."

"Fifty?" Eve asked, surprised.

"Yeah, he must have been some sort of Ex-Navy Seal or something," Adam murmured, eyes on his shoes.

"My God baby he must have been jacked!"

"Well not really," Adam began to stare intently at the amazing design in the rug. Never in Adam's life had his size failed him. His size was always there to back him up. His size always intimidated others. Now his size had failed him. He was not only ashamed by this but it also made him question who he was without his bulk. It made him question who he believed himself to be.

"So this guy with gray hair says, 'Attention is best' and then what happened Adam?"

"I don't know baby. It was just something about him that made me hate him. He seemed so confident and sure of himself, that everything in his world was a bed of roses and that everything worked out exactly the way he wanted it. It's kind of like when you see a gorgeous, I mean absolutely beautiful woman walk down the street and you just hate her for it. You hate her for all that she has and that you can never have! Have you ever seen something so beautiful that you just wanted to smash it; like that beauty never had the right to exist? Because it was so beautiful it made you feel so incredibly ugly. Have you ever felt that way?"

"Uh sort of," Eve's face reflected the discomfort she felt in regards to what Adam just said. "So, he was so handsome you wanted to hurt him?"

"Not handsome Evelyn, but so confident, so, perfect for lack of a better word. When I saw him look at me and say, 'Attention is best,' it made me snap. When I saw the way he carried himself it made me feel like such a loser. A feeling I haven't experienced since I got cut from ball. And I just snapped."

He shrugged and shifted his shoulders, turning his head as he thought about it. "You know that I am not a violent man. But those words and how he said them were like a rusty nail ripping through my mind."

Adam paused, and when he spoke again the words came rushing out. "You know what it was? He looked at me like a child. He looked at me like I was not a man. Like I was some little boy and he was a man's man. And you know babe, people just don't look at me that way. I am 6' 5" and 280 lbs, I demand respect. And those piercing eyes and slight smile were not showing me the respect that I deserve. And then that temper of mine boiled over and I swung at him."

"You threw a punch," Eve asked, shocked, "at a 50-year-old man who merely said, 'Attention is best'?"

"See, you do not understand. He was not merely a 50-year-old man. He was my job, my life, all the things that I never achieved. My life was fun at one point, it had meaning – and now it does not. So I threw the punch and then I thought I was going to die."

Adam looked at his wife. He looked at her like it was the first time that he had ever seen her. It finally imprinted upon his soul, he could have died today. If that man had wanted to, he could have ended his life and the impact of that brought him to tears. He saw the little brown fleck in his wife's blue eyes. He had never seen it before in the 10 years they had been married and now it was in front of him as clear as day. He was 38 years old and so much of his life had already flown by. He could hardly remember any of it. Often times he dreamt that he was still in college. That there were still term papers due or reports to write. Life was so simple then. Sometimes he would wake up and still think he was in Texas. Life had totally zoomed by. Where did it go? Now the enormity of his life, or lack thereof, hit him hard. By his own emotions, his own anger, he might have died today without ever seeing the fleck in his wife's eye. What had he become?

Our society puts a heavy burden on a big man. A big man is built to carry and support a lot of weight, not only on the shoulders but in his emotions as well. The bigger the man the less apt he is to cry. But when he does cry it is a sight that all stop to observe. Adam began to cry and cry. He cried not because he almost died but the realization that the majority of his life thus far had been lost. He was waking up to his miserable career, which poured onto his life. He was waking up to the realization that he had a business that he fit his life around. He was waking up to the fact that his life almost ended on the way to a client appointment, an appointment with a client that he did not even like.

"Baby, its okay. Its okay, I am here for you." Evelyn came over to him, putting an arm around his shoulders and running her fingers across his scalp as she hugged him to her belly.

Seeing a big man comforted by his petite loving wife is a beautiful thing. It is a thing of contrasts: the small comforting the large. It seems it should be the other way around but alas it is not.

Adam could not get the thought of his death out of his mind, knowing that it was all going to end. It was never a secret, but now he knew, really knew, just like the smoker who shrugs off the obvious, thinking their lungs are healthy until the moment the diagnosis comes… now suddenly it was so real. There was no such thing as immortality. Sure he had family that died but they were old. He was wrestling with all the emotions he had experienced today. What would have happened to his family if he had died? Would his boys have grown up the way he dreamed they would? Had he been a good father? Husband?

He remembered back in college in psych class that parents were the model of their child's behavior. He read that kids picked up the traits and patterns of their parents. Would his kids be just like him? A guy who worked all the time, doing things he did not like to do with people he did not like so he could have money to squeeze in a few activities with those that he loved?

A question pounded the inside of his skull. 'WHAT AM I DOING WITH MY LIFE?'

Chapter 5

Why Adam goes back to the bar.

Adam still felt out of kilter from the run-in with the gray-haired, blue-eyed man on the steps of the Landmark Tavern. But it was another day, once again dragging himself into work. Things did not seem to make much sense anymore. As he lumbered down the hall towards his office, his collar unbuttoned and his tie askew, Adam realized that he had forgotten to stop at Starbucks for his double latte. He never forgot his stop at Starbucks. As a proud stockholder, he liked to rationalize his four-dollar habit as an investment in his retirement. For Adam, coffee was vital to his morning well-being. "Damn it," he murmured to himself. "Where is my mind?"

As he said this the man's words once again wormed into his consciousness. "Attention is best." This triggered a cacophony of thoughts, 'What did he mean when he said that to me? Why did he say that to me? Who was that guy?'

At that moment, with the thoughts swimming in his head, Adam turned toward the break room for a cup of what passed for coffee at Talbot Securities. It was less a decision than an impulse, but if he had thought about it, he would have known he would later regret drinking it. Adam knew that the owners of the company bought the cheapest coffee known to mankind. He even suspected that the grinds were recycled – it certainly tasted no better than one imagines piss might.

He plodded towards the break room with his head down, lost in thought, muttering the man's words over and over. As he walked through the door, he crashed into Brian Craig, spilling Brian's coffee on his new cashmere sweater.

"Damn, Adam. Act on what you're saying, man. Pay attention" muttered an exasperated Brian. Brian Craig had been the top producer for Talbot Securities for the last 20 years. He was a legend in the industry, often quoted in the Wall Street Journal. He was rarely in the office, instead he spent most of his time traveling the world with his clients. And much to the amazement of his peers he only had a small number of clients. Craig's philosophy was to go deep with his relationships instead of wide. "I am in the office one time this month and you manage to ruin my favorite sweater."

"I, I'm sorry Brian." Adam yelped. "It's just that I have so much on my mind right now."

"Jeez, you look like a sad dog. You said attention is best. And no doubt it is." Brian said with a smile and a semi-nod of frustration.

"Yeah, that is what I am trying to figure out." Adam stood absorbing most of the break room with his hands in his pockets, shaking his head as if the movement might clear his thoughts.

"It's funny, you know, that's one of the greatest lessons my old teacher shared with me many years ago." Brian looked up and crossed his arms, and honored his teacher's memory with a half smile.

"Yeah? Some guy ran into me on the stairs of the Landmark Tavern and said 'Attention is best' and then savagely attacked me, nearly killing me." Adam puffed up with pride in remembering his survival and in the next moment rolled his shoulders forward and caved in from recalling what he survived – an assault from an old man.

"One guy nearly killed you Adam?" Brian asked incredulously. Adam was at least 7 inches taller than Brian and outweighed him by at least 100 lbs. Brian was amazed that anyone would ever mess with the behemoth of Adam Arbor. He often thought how appropriate his last name was given that he was a sequoia of a man.

"I could not believe it." Adam kept his eyes locked on his shoes as he confessed to Brian. "He must have been an ex-Navy Seal or something."

"Hmmph, and he said attention is best?"

Brian had a faraway look, as if he was trying to process something he didn't quite believe. He seemed to have forgotten about the coffee staining his sweater, standing with one hand resting under his chin, propped by his other arm.

"Yeah," Adam replied, nodding his head as in silent agreement with this attacker's nuttiness.

Brian asked, "Isn't the Landmark Tavern pretty close to Upton Street?"

Adam nodded.

"Damn, I haven't been in that area for about 20 years. I imagine it hasn't cleaned up much. He said 'Attention is best'? Those were his exact words?"

"Uh-huh, those were his exact words." Adam's eyes were wide, looking for Brian to sympathize with him.

"Did he have piercing blue eyes?" Brian pointed at his own and squinted to drive home the look that his teacher would sometimes give him.

"Yes, why?" Adam asked, suddenly beginning to comprehend that Brian might know the identity of his attacker. His jaw began to drop.

"About 6 foot?" Brian indicated a place just below Adam's nose with the flat of his hand. Adam looked down at the hand under his chin in embarrassment.

"Yes." Adam's pulse began to race and he shifted his bulk from foot to foot.

"Holy shit Adam! It sounds like you ran into Shane Tavaar! I can't believe it. What a great man." Brian paused, thinking. "Nah, it can't be him, but that is where the old dojo used to be." He trailed off into a conversation inside his head, reliving memories.

"You mean to tell me that you know him?" Adam's voice betrayed schoolgirl shock as he pressed against the wall, his body seeking protection.

"Know him?" Brian's face lit up with a flash of teeth. "Man, he used to be a great friend of mine. He was my old sensei and business coach. He helped me create my business when I was studying Ketsugo jujutsu with him. Must've been, let's see, about 25 years ago."

"You have to be kidding me." Adam swung his head slowly from side to side as if Brian's words were punches that snapped his chin from shoulder to shoulder.

"Shane Tavaar." Brian shook his head with pleasure. "What an amazing man!" A smile of remembered joy and respect flowed across his face.

"An amazing man?" An insulted Adam spitted, "that psycho nearly killed me!"

"No way man, he was just trying to teach a lesson." Brian laughed, "if he wanted to kill you, you would have been dead before you realized it."

Adam slumped slightly forward, acknowledging that Brian was right.

"He has, or had, a dojo about three blocks away from the Landmark, on Upton Street in a basement. We used to train there and after class I would buy him a beer so I could soak up as much of his wisdom as possible. He would talk to me about my business and how the art he was teaching applied to my rookie days here."

"He helped you create your business?" Adam needed a drink. This was too much to process so he grabbed a cup of corporate coffee. It wasn't whiskey, but tasted just as awful at the moment. "Affluence with hardly any time in the office and a business that is effortless! Man, I would kill for your kind of business Brian!"

"Yeah, without him I wouldn't have ever been a top producer at this firm. It's thanks to Tavaar that I am still the number one guy. Not that it matters, but I do what I do because it's my Way." As Brian talked, his countenance became peaceful, as one does when he knows who he is, or when someone comes home after a long journey.

"Your **way**?" Adam's head tilted as his curiosity was tickled. There had been something in how Brian spoke that hinted at more than the words themselves.

"Mmm. Tavaar introduced me to that concept. It's from Ketsugo jujutsu. The samurai used to call it Bushido. In Tavaar's terms he referred to it as Bujutsu, or way. He would call it the way of the warrior."

"The way of the warrior? In the 21st-century business world? How does samurai crap apply to today's world?"

Brian looked at him for what seemed like minutes before he spoke. "Maybe it's that attitude which attracted Tavaar into your world. Maybe you're looking for a way."

"What?"

"I bet he mentioned that there was no such thing as coincidences."

"How did you know?" Adam stammered. This revelation was overwhelming Adam's ability to process. Brian Craig was the firm's absolute biggest producer. Adam had always admired Brian and wanted to be like him. Now he was discovering that the person who almost killed him, who made him doubt his own identity, was his hero's teacher.

"I was a student of his for a long time. Like I said, he was the guy that made me. I wouldn't be where I am in business if not for him."

"So this martial arts guy helps you build a multi-million dollar business?" Adam crossed his arms, as if to block this nonsense coming from Brian's mouth.

"Oh, yeah. That and much more Adam. There was a lot to Tavaar. Martial arts expert, a successful entrepreneur. He traveled, lectured around the world, even wrote a few books, I think. Back in the day he was the guru's guru and then one day he just disappeared. He was gone without a trace, I went to the dojo and it was closed with a note and a poem on the door. All it said was that he would be back but not to wait for him. I remember it almost exactly… that each of us was now to find our own paths guided by the knowledge he had shared with us. I will never forget that day." There was a faraway look in Brian's eyes. "God, I felt so empty and shallow, like I was utterly alone knowing that my teacher was no longer there." He paused, and thrust his hands into his pockets, rocking on his heels. "But you know, as time passed I realized he never left me and that he is still with me even to this day. That is why I never went to search for him. Because he never left."

The two men lapsed into silence, Brian lost in thought, Adam waiting for something more. Finally, he asked "What was the poem?"

"Oh, it wouldn't make sense to you. Adam, you crossed paths with an exceptional human being. You have to take to heart that it was not a coincidence. Maybe this sounds like nonsense to you right now, but on some level this is a test for you and your future. When I look around this place and watch you walk into the office, it's pretty obvious to me that you aren't happy here and that you feel stuck in your business. Tavaar used to tell us the universe wants you to succeed. It wants you to evolve to your highest level and it is constantly providing the opportunities for that evolution but unfortunately we are often unconscious to the many teachers and circumstances provided to accelerate us. This could be a massive wake-up call for you Adam. Or it could simply be a random run in with a blue-eyed, gray-haired crazy man. It might sound trite, but I mean this – the choice is yours just as it always has been and will ever be."

"Jeez, Brian, you are getting pretty deep here. It's kind of scaring me."

"Adam, I've had some great teachers and Tavaar was one of them. He disappeared from my life about 20 years ago and now he appears in yours. Makes you wonder why. He must see something in you, or sensed something about you and that is why the both of you met."

"Huh?" Adam snorted.

"Don't try to understand it. Tavaar used to tell me, 'it takes time for rice to cook.' I've gotta take my sweater to the dry cleaner and catch a plane. I won't be back in the office for another six weeks as I'm going to Tuscany to learn to cook with some of my top clients. You just remember this: Tavaar is an amazing man. What you do with that is up to you. The only thing I can do is wish you luck. Hey, if you see do him again, send him my love and gratitude."

Brian turned away, pulling off his sweater as he walked down the hall. Watching him go, Adam took another drink of coffee. With disgust, he looked down at what was left of the vile stuff in his cup as he pondered his friend's words.

Chapter 6

Herb Fay

The collision with Brian Craig churned in Adam's mind as he sat behind his desk. A thought bubbled, 'The blue-eyed man said there were no accidents. Was my spilling of Brian's coffee an accident? It's not like I meant to do it, but it still happened. And if I hadn't spilled it I wouldn't have learned about this guy Tavaar.' Adam shook his head. 'No, it had to be an accident. What else could it have been?'

Adam, lost in thought in his office, hands behind his head, had his gaze fixed upon the ceiling tiles when Herb Fay strutted by his office. Adam's blank stare attracted Fay's attention.

"That kind of activity," Herb chirped, "will never get you more ceiling tiles; keep it up, and you are doomed to a life of mediocrity – and you will never get an office like mine." There was a smugness to Fay's voice; his office was by far the biggest in the firm. Worse still, he was the kind of man who was proud of his ceiling tile count. He basked in the fact that he had 33% more than his nearest colleague. Not so strange given that he was the branch manager and had been with the firm 25 years, but weird in that during renovations, Fay had demanded design changes in the building layout to maximize the number of tiles in his office. Specifically, he had one of his walls extended to purposely minimize Brian's tile count. That wasn't public knowledge of course, even though he liked to trumpet the end fact. Herb was a firm believer in stacking the deck to win by any means necessary.

"What?" Adam shifted in his chair and swung his massive head towards the peacock whose squawk had interrupted his deep meditation. Although he never said it, Adam often wondered why his boss had never noticed that such a source of pride could disappear simply by putting in smaller tiles in another office.

"You know as well as I do, Adam, that size matters. Size is indicative of success. The bigger your office is, the bigger your house is, the bigger your watch is, the more successful you are! It shouts out to all that you know and don't know that you have made it." Herbs' eyes bulged with emphasis. "That you're a somebody! A person not to be trifled with! And bigness is a matter of sales success!" Fay grinned and did his proverbial watch flip so others could tell the time on his watch. "You see this watch?" and ramrod straight he stood with his index finger pointing at the watch. His face was caught in an open mouth grin and his eyes entranced by the gleam of platinum and diamonds of the slug of precious metal on his wrist.

Adam nodded. He had seen this routine thousands of times. He could almost recite every word that Herb was about to utter about the greatness of his watch and hence himself.

"This is a Rolex Presidente, and look how it commands your respect! Look how it awes you and puts you in your proper place. Look how it tells the story of his owner: successful, commanding, knowledgeable, a Lothario, gastronome and defender of the environment. I just need to allow my clients a mere glimpse of this Teutonic sculpture and they're awed into submission to my will. This is only one arrow in my quiver of success, but it helps me sell as much and have all that I have. Another is my $200 ascot – not a tie, an ascot – tells the story of refinement. Look how refined I seem. People see the package, and they think 'there's a man of discriminating tastes and obviously an expert at what he does.'" Herb finished his monologue with a theatrical lowering of his watch to his side.

"Obviously," Adam threw in.

"Arbor, when are you going to wake up and start producing to your potential? You have plenty of talent. You remind me of me when I was your age except that Herb Fay was more motivated." He poked an index finger in the air to emphasize his point. "Your sales have been flat for the last 3 years. You had such a great start. What happened to you, Adam? Beyond getting fat and lazy?"

Adam scowled, and anger flared across his face.

"I meant that purely figuratively Adam. You still look in great shape." Fay said with a semi-sneer.

"Arbor, I'm saying this with a lot of love so please don't take it wrong. You know damn well that I have a vested interest in you growing your business. When you make money I make money. You need to do more Adam, more calls, more seminars, more appointments, more direct mail, more email, and more ads. You need to do more so you can have more because when you have more you want to do more! Nothing motivates like a $20,000 dollar watch or an $8,000 mortgage payment. Do you know what my nut is each month that I have to cover? If I don't push myself every day I'm not going to survive the month. And I love it. It keeps me alive! It keeps me sharp! Fight for survival every day, or you stagnate and get fat. That's what I see you forgetting, Adam. You aren't challenging yourself. You are fat, happy and complacent. Third place or the bronze metal is good enough for you. You've become a damn half-stepper. You need to take action to live up to that potential so you can have a watch like mine, a house like mine and even a satisfied wife like mine."

"A satisfied wife?" Adam was taken aback by the last comment. He was used to Herb's addiction to material success and had slowly become calloused to that type of motivation, but Adam was sensitive about his relationship with his wife.

"Do you really think Eve is satisfied with what you have provided for her?"

Adam was dumbfounded.

"You aren't providing as much as you could. Buy her stuff. Show her what a great provider you are. Show her how much of a man you are. If you give her more you will get more. As a matter of fact I have always thought she is cute. Do you mind if I buy her something?" Herb's voice trailed off with a covetous glance.

Adam glared, his eyes smoldering over the adulterous innuendo, his mouth tightened into a thin line of rage.

"No offense, Adam. You can always buy something for Ivanka. Maybe that's what it will take to motivate you, a beautiful 24-year old Estonian with expensive tastes!" Herb adjusted his ascot as he waited for Adam's reply. The man clearly knew the bait he had thrown out. Despite his calm demeanor, his eyes belied a malicious intent behind his comments.

"Get out!" Adam could barely contain his temper. He rose from his desk and moved toward Fay.

"That's it Adam! Get angry! Use that anger to get your sales to the next level. Use that spark of motivation! Perhaps it will help you get some more tiles!" With that parting comment Herb continued his parade around the building, leaving Adam to stand awkwardly, fuming.

Chapter 7

Good enough for Brian, good enough for Adam

Adam was mad as he sat back down. Fay always got his goat. 'That little ascot-wearing prick. Buy Eve a gift to show her what a provider he is. What a man he is. Christ.' Adam sighed and mumbled, "Herb, and his frigging watch," but behind that he wondered why he was not as motivated as he used to be. Where had the fire gone? When had he come to think his business was boring? Same thing, day in and day out. Make phone calls, make appointments, see people, run proposals, repeat the process: the corporate treadmill.

He pushed his heft back from the desk, looked up to count his changeless ceiling tiles and wondered why? 'Why do I do this? Why do I choose to spend my life doing this?' Adam slowly scanned his office taking in all his plaques, trophies, pictures and the corporate detritus. His view of his vast accomplishments made him sigh and surrender his head to the coldness of his desk. As his anger began to ebb, Adam launched into the never-ending dialog a man has with himself about things that only matter to that individual man.

He was seeking the real meaning behind his life. He made more than enough money, had a great house, a great wife and healthy wonderful children, but these things still seemed never to be enough. He knew that there had to be something else out there, and he felt guilty about being totally unmotivated to go out and get it. Adam lifted his head and sighed. 'I don't want to get on the phone and make more calls or make appointments. God, I'm tired. Tired of the pro-verbial 'more' conversation. More for what? Why should I do more? Why build my business if it's only going to lead to more suffering?' He was tired of waiting for someday, when he had enough money to be happy. Did he want money? He wanted clarity, clarity about his desires, a clear sense of what his life was about. He hoped that someday it would work out but he had no idea how. He had held tightly to this hope from his early childhood and yet deep down Adam was still wondering.

He looked backed to his tiles for guidance. 'Yep, still 108 tiles' he reminded himself. Something about Fay's status monologue continued to resonate, Adam realized. He knew he wanted to make more money but he also knew he wasn't motivated to go out and build what he did again. He knew that if he doubled his business it would be lucrative, but he also was certain that doing so the same way he built up what he had would kill him.

Adam's body sagged, and he slumped back in his chair. He was not 22 years old and single anymore with the time and the gumption to start his day at 7am and end it at 9 at night, smiling, dialing and going on appointments. He also knew in his heart that if he did double his business he would not be able to handle it. Even now he felt tapped out with his production and the amount of work that he had to do just to maintain his current level of business, let alone grow it. He was trapped between wanting to grow his business and having to manage what he already had, and the trap had seemed particularly tight lately.

He thought enviously of Brian Craig and how effortless and fun his business seemed to be. For years it had continued to puzzle Adam how Brian always did better and yet never seemed to care what his business did or where his production was. Herb Fay never bothered Brian and yet Adam believed Herb was always in or on his ass needling him.

Adam looked to the wisdom of his tiles and thought with resignation and a little disgust, '9:30 in the morning, and I need a drink. Pathetic.' Then an epiphany interrupted his thoughts – 'if he is good for Brian Craig then he is good for me.'

In that moment, Adam Arbor began to feel like he had gained some clarity. He did not know how he was going to do it but he wanted more out of life and his business. He wanted the world of Brian Craig, not the domain of Herb Fay. He repeated to himself, "if this Tavaar guy is good enough for Brian Craig then he is good enough for me. Perhaps it was not an accident I collided with that guy." He was committed to finding out.

Chapter 8

A moth to flame

What draws a moth to a flame? A moth never plunges into the fire directly but will circle the hurricane lamp in tighter and tighter concentric loops. Once it has locked on to the light it will pound itself against the glass to reach its nirvana.

Adam kept circling the neighborhood which contained the Landmark Tavern. He found excuses to go to the restaurants in the neighborhood. He changed his dry cleaner to be closer to the tavern, as if he were an alcoholic looking to stay close to home. But Adam was seeking a catalyst. He scouted the area, convincing himself of his commitment. He wanted to know where he was going, so that getting lost would not be an excuse to back out. For days he had been thinking about his encounter with Brian Craig, and he was intrigued by what Craig had said about Tavaar.

Adam thought back to his football days and the grueling practices. As a defensive lineman he loved to lift weights but hated to run. His coaches knew this so they made him do extra wind sprints; it wasn't until game days, when he still had wind in the fourth quarter, that he understood the wisdom of the extra conditioning. He remembered his coach yelling:

"Arbor you ever seen the Olympics?"

"Yes, Coach."

"So you know that they have gold, silver and bronze medals." His words were punctuated with tobacco juice slipping down the side of his chin.

"Yes, Coach."

"And the difference between those medal winners is often 100th's of a second." He emphasized his point by holding up two meaty fingers showing a small gap between them.

"Yes, Coach."

"So a little itty bitty difference can make a huge impact, right?"

"I guess so?"

"Well Arbor, who do you think makes more money with sponsorships, their face on the Wheaties box, all that crap?" The coach barked with his hands on his hips.

"Ahhh, the gold medal winners."

"That's right Arbor. In practice today I want you to be aware of what medal you are playing for. Is second or third place good enough for you? It's fractions that make a world of a difference, so practice like you mean it. Earn your gold medal! When you're running wind sprints today, you're running for the gold. Small difference, huge pay off, Arbor! Remember that and get running!"

It had been decades since Adam had thought about that day, yet now his coach's words were very clear to him. He knew he needed someone to push him, someone to help him shave those tenths of a second off his sprint. Was Tavaar someone who could help him do it? Would Tavaar even bother to help him?

One afternoon, Adam found himself standing at the bottom of the stairs at the Landmark Tavern, his dry cleaning slung over his shoulder and his eyes on the intersection of Hamm and Center Street. Looking at those stairs caused him to sweat, since they triggered the memory of his bulk failing him. It seemed like that day had revealed who he truly was. He was not intimidating, just a scared boy trying to find his way, and this man Tavaar saw through the façade. Not only did he see through the veneer but he forced Adam to confront his vulnerability. In a moment's time, Tavaar had shattered his illusions, and now Adam found himself back where the seismic event of his life had happened.

"Attention is best" howled through his head, and "do not be under the illusion that we met accidentally."

There is little physiological distinction between fear and anticipation; one or both were welling up inside Adam as he stared at the door of the Landmark. He was having difficulty interpreting the parallel sensations. Adam was confident that Brian Craig would not recommend or introduce him to anyone who could hurt him but he was still apprehensive of the intensity of Tavaar.

As he stood below the door gazing intently with his head slightly cocked to the side, a conversation erupted within the bookends of his ears:

'What am I doing here? This is stupid. Do I really think someone can help me get as lucky as Brian Craig? He's got everything going for him. What do you got going for you? Brian is blessed. I, on the other hand, well that's a point open for contention. What if this guy tries to hurt me again and this time does? I should get out of here, he might come out at any moment. Man, I wish my wife was here because I would feel safer.'

His mind continued to rattle, like a BB in an empty beer can in the hands of a five year old. It bounced from one negative point to another, and finally ended with outlandish thoughts.

'What if Herb sees me here? Maybe this guy is in the mafia? I wonder if I am dressed properly? I wonder what he will think of my shoes? I hope my watch is shouting the right message.' It was that statement that stopped the rattling BB. 'Oh my God,' Adam thought to himself. 'I just quoted that bastard Herb Fay.' Adam's disgust pulled him back under control, and with the thought of Herb Fay in his mind, he walked up and pushed open the door.

Chapter 9

Over the threshold

The door swung open with the push of Adam's meaty hand. Oak, dimness, the dust floating in the cones of light over round tables guarded by high stools, the shine of brass and the long wooden bar filled his awareness. It was an old bar, a place that had been frequented by all kinds for many years, and yet it still held vibrancy. There was energy here and Adam felt it. Maybe the energy filling this place was not from the place but from the man at the far end of the bar. He was sitting tall and erect yet relaxed with his back to the bar and his eyes soft, looking out the window with a dark beer in his hand.

When Adam saw him his heart leapt into his throat and he felt a fine mist of sweat surface on his back, much like the instant dampness that is generated when you are in the wilderness and you see a wild predator in its habitat. To Adam, the man was like a bear that he had already run into, so he had a much deeper respect for what that bear could do. It's like a wave of fear and awe crashing on the individual at the same time, to be fearfully fascinated. As when any of us see a wolf in the wild our first instinct is to freeze, which is exactly what Adam did.

He froze in the doorway like a rabbit. With his dry cleaning thrown over his shoulder he just stared at the man. It was a stare of a jangled response. Adam did not expect Tavaar to be here. It was momentous enough just to walk up the stairs and push open the door but now the man was actually here. It is one thing to hear a noise in the garage and get up the gumption to go investigate it. It is quite another feeling to investigate the garage and discover that there is someone in it! He thought to himself, 'shit what do I do now?'

Tavaar slowly turned towards the door and, seeing this huge rabbit of a man hiding in plain sight, locked his eyes on Adam. What was always slightly unnerving about Tavaar was that when he looked at you, he really looked at you. His eyes would just watch and absorb you. No judgment, no breaking away of eye contact because he did not want you to know that you were looking at him. When he looked at you he really looked at you and he noticed. Sometimes it felt like he looked at you and knew everything about you at the same time. His gaze was completely open; he looked at you to learn, to absorb you and your being without hostility, only an innate curiosity.

Adam on the other hand was a tad disturbed by his look. He had seen it before when Tavaar's hand was sticking out of his throat. An amazingly keen intelligence without an agenda, a gaze bent on absorption instead of judgment, like a scientist looking at a slide under a microscope. In a word: curious.

What happens in the space between two people before they meet? Possible futures get played out in the minds of the participants and if a future is viable enough they take the next step forward. Sometimes if one person is intimidating or scary the meeting gets avoided, or if they do not meet the criteria on the list the meeting does not happen. Most criteria lists are unconscious to most people, but we run through them without fully recognizing what we're doing: Are they dangerous? Do they smell? Will they like me? Can they help me? Do they fit my client profile? Do they have money? Are they funny? Are they single? Is their costume appropriate? Will they make me better off?

All of these questions and more were firing in Adam's head. The most compelling one was that Adam knew that this man was dangerous, that he could hurt him. He knew from Brian Craig that this man used to be one of those kung fu combat black belt teachers somewhere in the belly of the city, but competing with the fear conversation was the vision of what Craig had created and it was this man who helped him do it.

He made his choice, motivated by what would seem to be a world-shifting step, Adam strode across the room, sputtering "Hello" as he stuck his hand out in front of him like a blind man's cane looking for the curb to protect its user from an awkward fall into traffic.

"Hello," Tavaar responded. "have you figured it out?

"What's that?"

"That attention is best."

"So you do recognize me."

"Yes, and I am amused that you have found your way back here. Most people that I share things with are not interested in more."

"You have an interesting way of sharing."

"I know. It works every now and then." Tavaar maintained his handshake and continued to look into Adam's eye. He never got up from the stool but had turned his body to face Adam. Adam's figure towered over Tavaar but Tavaar carried himself as if he were playing with a puppy or a small child. Adam was acutely aware that Tavaar had not even considered the possibility that Adam's size could be of any threat to him.

When we look back at our lives from the rocker on the porch we remember moments. Often a few very vivid moments stand out where the paths of our lives shifted or the path we were traveling on suddenly forked and took an unexpected turn stand out. And it is those moments that we look back upon from the future, the ones about which we can say, it was in that moment that our life shifted.

A friend of Adam's had once told him about the moment he decided to get married, and the moment five years later when the marriage had ended. "It was the strangest thing," he'd said. "We were walking in the University's botanical gardens late one afternoon. Sun was up still, perfect kind of day. We're in the area where they have three or four acres of tall grass prairie. I don't know if you've been there, but from the paths through the grass, about the only part of town you can see are some dark red brick buildings, about 6-7 stories tall. Well, we're walking along and the sunlight is kind of yellow on these buildings, turning their color so that it reminds me of the desert out west. And I look down at her, and I'm suddenly in this scene where we're walking on a real prairie, and there are two little boys in overalls, short blond crewcuts, barefoot, running around as we watch them play. I knew right then that I would marry her. It was the first time in my life ever, that I had seen myself as a father, and she was there. She was the one, the mother of my boys. I was awestruck, wondering what had gotten into me. I still don't understand it. Why would I have had that vision? I'd been in love before, but never had that thought."

He sighed and was silent for a few moments. When he resumed, there was an air of frustration and sorrow in his voice. "And then you know, you actually get married, the years start to go by, you see the differences between you. We moved after grad school, you know, out east, and I took a job that just seemed

56

perfect. It was really engaging, occupied my thoughts all the time. After a while, I felt less and less like we had things in common, especially since she was kind of spinning her wheels professionally. She was doing some teaching, but it didn't really engage her and she mostly complained about it. It was no fun, man, I'm telling ya', but I wasn't the kind of person who gets divorced. I just wasn't, I thought that was only for other people. So I went along, trying to make the best of things. She's doing the same. Meanwhile, we haven't had kids, we aren't even talking about it. One day I come home from work, and she tells me that she's walking down the hall at school and overhears one of the other teachers. He's telling his daughter that he and her mother are getting divorced, and that he's going to start dating one of the other teachers. Sixteen year old kid, student at the school, being told in the hall by her dad that he's leaving her mom and taking up with her music teacher. Can you believe that shit?"

He shook his head. "You know my wife's telling me this, and I'm thinking to myself what a lousy thing to do to your kid, but then suddenly I said to myself 'my god, that could be me in fifteen or twenty years. Do I really want to be overheard telling my teenager I'm leaving his mom?' And you know, I didn't want that to be me. The whole thing, I learned in listening to her tell that story, I am the kind of person who gets divorced. And we did." There was a long silence, and then he lifted his beer glass and said, "Adam, let's talk about something else."

With marriage, it's not the ceremony, but that moment when something shifted in us to commit to this person as our spouse, and many times it's a simple innocuous moment where providence shifts. Sometimes we recognize it in that moment, sometimes we don't, but with reflection it sticks out with clarity.

Now, in a "hello" and a handshake, Adam's path had forked.

"My name is Adam Arbor and a friend of mine, Brian Craig told me about you."

"Brian Craig? That is a name I have not heard for some time." Tavaar leaned back and remembered with his eyes; a smile cracked across his face. "How is he?"

"He is doing quite well. He's been the top producer in our office for as long as I have worked there."

Tavaar just nodded and agreed with his head. His reaction was that it was expected that he would be the top producer, much like it is expected that the ocean is salty.

"Well, you obviously know that my name is Shane Tavaar. So how can I be of service to you?"

"Can I buy you a drink?" asked Adam and with a few words the process began.

Tavaar nodded and motioned for Adam to take the stool next to him.

"So what brought you here, Adam?" inquired Tavaar. "And why do you want to meet me?"

Adam took a few moments to speak. He didn't want to rush, but he had a lot to say. "You did something to me, Tavaar. Ever since I ran into you, my life's changed. You made me doubt all that I considered to be me. My size never failed me before, and yet you schooled me in a matter of moments. My size and strength were useless. I had never been rendered helpless before." Adam cleared his throat and took a swallow of whiskey. He stared into his glass at the ice before again looking at Tavaar. "Sitting there on those steps at your mercy made me think about what I was doing with my life and my business. At some level it felt as if I was jolted awake, that I had to face something, or admit something, that I never had before.

"In that one moment, I realized that I was mortal that at any moment my life could end or be ended by something or someone like you. I didn't like the picture I saw. I was spending too much of my life doing things with and for people I don't really like; I was chasing a will-o'-the-wisp, trying to be a success, to get wealthy, to get people to respect who I am. And in that moment when you said attention is best I realized what I had been paying attention to was a waste of time. That I was tired of all the things I was tired from, so I took a swing in frustration at what you represented to me. Everything that I did not have, yet wanted, like peace and success. I suppose at the moment I did not realize all of this but the more I've thought about it, that is what has been coming up for me. Honestly, Tavaar, I haven't thrown a punch in anger at someone since I was 12 years old, 26 years ago."

Tavaar was watching Adam, and listening attentively. "Sometimes the universe pushes the evolve button a little faster than we expect but we must have faith," he whispered.

"What?" Adam asked quizzically.

He shook his head. "Go on, go on. Sometimes an old man like me mutters."

Adam didn't know whether Tavaar was serious, but he continued. "I guess my run-in with you forced me to think and reflect on who I am and what I am doing, not to mention the pressure work is putting on me. My career has stagnated; I keep making the same amount of money no matter how hard or how little I work. It's like I am on auto pilot at work. I want more but I am always so busy managing and trying to figure out what I have. I know that I have a great life to anyone looking in. I am married to a great woman, 2 wonderful kids, a nice house, I wear nice suits, I have a nice German car. Everything is nice. Hell, people even describe me as a nice guy but I know there has to be more. But I am busy and I do not know what else to do and to me there has to be more in this world than just nice."

"So at work I literally ran into Brian Craig, and spilled his coffee all over him. He's a guy who has it all. He makes more and more money every year, he's rarely in the office, and he's more than nice. He is alive. It is so effortless for him. Brian Craig emanates life. Well, we're talking and I tell him about our encounter, and he gives me your name and says that you're an amazing teacher." Adam paused and took another swallow of whiskey. "I sit here and look at you, and I can see that you're alive too, and that whatever Brian has, he learned from you. So I came back here because I want more, Tavaar. I want to be like Brian Craig, and you are the key."

Up to that moment, Tavaar had been motionless on the barstool, watching Adam and listening to his story. But as Adam finished, Tavaar looked down at his glass, raised and drained it in a gulp, and pushed back to stand up.

"Hmm, I worked with Brian many years ago when I developed men for a living but that time has long passed. I no longer help men who want. I'm sorry Adam, it was a pleasure to meet you. Thanks for the drink, but I can't help you."

"Wait. What do you mean by want?"

"There is a distinction between wanting and committing. You may want a better business and life, but are you committed? Are you really willing?"

"Yes, yes I am!"

"Hmm." Tavaar looked at Adam, seeming to appraise him. "We shall see. I am here every Thursday at 5. Let's see how committed you are. Meet me here next week at 5 and if you are buying, I am drinking."

"Really? You will help me really?"

"Perhaps. If you meet me here at 5 next week, I will begin to see if you are committed or not. Are you committed to meeting me here at 5 next Thursday, Adam?"

"Yes, I am Tavaar."

"Well then, I will honor your commitment."

Chapter 10

A five game series

Adam was giddy with excitement. It was as if he had been infected with the disease of hope. He had a teacher, someone who would help him make sense of his world and rejuvenate his interest in the business. His entire work week flowed. It seemed that just the thought of meeting with Tavaar made his business and life happen effortlessly. Thursday came, and Adam kept his eye on his watch, waiting for 4:30 when he would begin his trek to the Landmark Tavern. He knew he could get there in about 20 minutes, but he wanted to be early for his first meeting. It would be his first opportunity to create a world like Brian Craig has.

The first meeting

Adam took the stairs of the tavern three at a time, excited and eager, believing in his heart that his life was about to begin to unfold in a new way. It was finally his opportunity to create what he always wanted: peace, prosperity and a feeling of accomplishment. The key was this man Tavaar, who had so jangled his world. The one who had made him doubt his size, his strength and his invulnerability. As his eyes adjusted to the light inside, he looked about the tavern and saw that Tavaar was not there yet. He glanced at his watch: "4:57, I am three minutes early."

He sat down at the bar and ordered a beer. As the barkeep placed the frosty glass in front of him he heard the tavern door swing open. He instinctively looked at his watch – 5 p.m. – and in walked Shane Tavaar.

"Adam, it's good to see you. You're on time, just like you promised. Thank you. I'll have a Guinness." Adam looked at Tavaar as a boy does when he brings home straight A's to show his parents. Reaching down into his attaché case, he pulled out a new and unopened spiral notebook while motioning to the bartender.

Tavaar gazed at the notebook and said, "Why Adam, you almost seem like you are committed to the adventure you're about to embark on with me. Interesting and very good." Tavaar raised the glass in front of him and sampled it. "You know, this beer is luscious. It's amazing how many flavors can be contained in a pint."

"So what are we going to talk about Tavaar?" Adam interjected.

"Talking? You may have noticed that the process has already begun. The real question is, are you ready?"

Shane looked at him in the way a sympathetic adult looks at a child when they say they will be a rock star when they grow up. Not discouragingly, but with keen interest, as if weighing the person's mettle. No one wants to shut down a young child's hopes, but responding kindly really requires judging how to respond; is this a kid who is capable of paying prices to become what they want to be? Everyone wants to be wealthy but most are not willing to act to achieve that goal.

Adam thought back over the week, how everything clicked. His business and his life flowed because he had made a commitment to meet Tavaar. He did not understand why that was but he did know that things were different.

As Adam began to answer, Tavaar tipped back his beer, finished it with a smile, got up and walked away. As he angled toward the door Adam interrupted his smooth gait, blurting out, "I thought we were going to talk about stuff so I can be more like Brian Craig?"

"We already did. I'll see you next week Adam."

Adam glanced at his watch. It was 5:12.

The second meeting

Once again Adam arrived at the tavern at 4:57, and Tavaar walked in promptly at 5 p.m. Adam had ordered already. On the bar was Tavaar's Guinness. Shane smiled and put his hand on the glass. In that moment when Tavaar touched the glass, his face relaxed and the muscles in his shoulders fell ever so slightly as he exhaled. It seemed that time actually froze in the tavern. All of Shane's attention was focused on the feel of the glass in his hand, the nudge of the bar plank's wood against his forearm. In his mind he took a moment to thank God for his life.

Adam on the other hand had already downed half his beer and begun hurtling questions and answers at Tavaar. "What should we do first to double my production? Do you think I should start hitting the phone harder. I think I am pretty good at sales so maybe we should start with how my office looks. But you know, I think it looks pretty good. I do have one of the largest offices in the complex. I'm up to 108 tiles, you know."

"Really." Adam didn't notice Tavaar's feigned attempt to seem impressed.

"One of the guys in the office heard of a guy who knew of a guy whose coach told him he should buy an expensive car so he looks the part. I do have a BMW already maybe I should upgrade to a Mercedes."

Tavaar just nodded his head, as if enjoying this spectacle of chatter.

Adam kept asking and answering his own questions. Tavaar attentively listened and enjoyed his Guinness.

Nodding once more, Tavaar raised his beer and looked at Adam. "I am impressed with you so far. Until next week." With a final sip, he stood up and turned to leave.

"Wait!" Adam was startled. "When I am going to start learning stuff?"

Tavaar smiled. "I am already teaching you more than you can comprehend at the moment, but with steadiness and a fixed purpose it will all become abundantly clear."

Adam tilted his head like a dog does when it's translating English into dog. "Huh?"

"Till next week Adam. And thanks for the beer."

"Uh, well I, uh, yeah, okay." Adam sat at the bar befuddled. What the hell was going on? He had left work early now for the second week in a row and he hadn't learned anything yet from this allegedly brilliant teacher and builder of business and men. 'Maybe this was a crock, maybe Brian Craig was just lucky and things just fell his way.' Adam turned to the barkeep and requested a Jack Daniels straight up, brooding over his confusion and disappointment.

The third meeting

Adam left the office at 4:40 this time. Doubt had plagued his mind all week. He wondered if this was the best use of his time. He could be spending this time more productively meeting with clients or going home to play with his kids. His mind would skip from doubt into hope. Deep down, Adam knew that if Brian Craig could have such an amazing life by design, with a successful business at the heart of it, so could he. Frankly, he realized that he knew of no-one else who might help him get there. It was as if the doubt and hope were mingled at times with despair.

Earlier in the day, Herb had tried to sell him on another opportunity for self-motivation, popping into Adam's office with a grin, saying, "Adam, you need to dig yourself into a bigger hole. You need to activate that fight or flight mechanism to see what you are made of! Look what I just did to keep myself fired up to produce and run you monkeys."

He pulled out a color brochure from his pocket and proudly displayed a picture of his new 48' boat. "Be impressed, Adam."

Fay looked at him expectantly and then said, "I have never owned a boat before. I only thought of it last week, you know."

Adam nodded. He'd been feeling down that morning, and this just made him feel worse. He could barely manage a smile inside when he wondered how many ceiling tiles were in the boat's cabin.

Fay seemed not to notice. Poking a finger in Adam's face, he said, "Sure, it's new, it's big, and I don't even really sail, but as my mom always said, if you're going to play why not play big!" Fay blustered, puffing himself up and hooking his thumbs in his lapels as he turned away and took a few steps for the door. When he turned back, he was wearing the face of a holier-than-thou street prophet.

"I think you need a boat Adam! Or maybe you and Eve can come for a little midnight sail!" Herb gave a sly wink that Adam had seen him give strippers at the Naked Eye when he tipped them a Benjamin after a lap dance, and bile rose to Adam's mouth.

Swallowing hard, Adam rose and grabbed his case. "Thanks, boss. I've got a meeting, but I'll think about what you said." He nearly ran past Fay to get out of the building for an hour.

On his way to the Landmark, Adam shook his head at the memory, praying to himself, 'please God, don't ever let me be like him.'

Perhaps because of his encounter with Fay that morning, Adam was eager to get to the tavern. He wanted to learn. In a strange way, even though he and Tavaar had not been talking about much he felt different about himself. On some level something was shifting inside of him. He could not describe the feeling with words yet, but he did know something was occurring.

As he swung open the tavern door once more, he checked his watch to find it was 4:59. As usual Tavaar had not arrived yet. He ordered and looked expectantly at the door, waiting for Tavaar to bound in. No Tavaar. Five minutes later, he was still waiting. "Hmm," he wondered out loud.

At 5:10, the bartender wandered over. "You're that guy who meets with Shane every Thursday about now, right?"

"Yeah, that's me."

"He told me to give you this at 5pm. Sorry I got tied up in some other things. The Missus is a little upset with me at the moment. You know how that is, right?" With a shrug, he handed Adam a piece of stationary emblazoned with an Old English 'T' on the top, and walked down the bar to help a group of women who had just come in. Adam could not help but notice the quality and feel of the paper as he called out a thanks to the bartender.

On the note in beautiful script it read:

> Adam, thank you for keeping your commitment. Your will is getting stronger. I hope it is strong enough. See you next week at 5.
>
> Be well,
>
> Shane

Adam looked at the note and read it three times, as if it might have meaning he couldn't find. Discouraged, he wondered yet again what he was doing. Was this just a pipedream? How could this make a difference in his business? In his life? In frustration Adam barked to the barkeep "Give me a shot of Jack and another beer."

The fourth meeting

From the moment Adam hit the snooze button that morning he was running late for everything he did. He had needed the sleep, but even a few extra minutes set him up to be late for his first client meeting of the day and things just snowballed from that point on. His coming meeting with Tavaar was about the one thing that salvaged a space for peace in his mind as his frustration mounted. He knew he had to be at that meeting and he did not want to be late, but he figured that Tavaar would understand. Sometimes a successful guy runs late, he said to himself more than once.

The day was flying by with this and that to do. At times Adam felt like a bee, perhaps accomplishing some work but mostly buzzing and buzzing some more because of his lateness. Busy, busy, busy just like a bee began to run through his mind, an annoying mantra. As he gathered his pollen for the day he stopped for a moment to look at his watch and it read 4:45. "Damn. Thursday and I'm going to be late."

Adam arrived at 5:02 to find Shane walking out the door and down the steps, a reversed encounter of their first meeting. Adam looked up as Tavaar brushed past. "Tavaar, where are you going?"

"Adam I told you before I no longer deal with men who only want. I only work with men who are committed."

"I am committed, Tavaar."

"No you are not." Tavaar stated flatly. "You are two minutes late."

"But I…."

Tavaar interrupted, "Please do not shower me with excuses. Until the day comes that you decide that you control your world and excuses do not exist, I'm not interested. Only then will I again consider teaching you." Tavaar's eyes were intent, holding Adam locked in his gaze. He continued quietly. "There are only two ways of being in this world, Adam. You are either late or early. The probability of you arriving on time anywhere is relatively nil. To be on time is deeper than you seem to understand. There is a one-second moment of time, so choose what kind of person you want to be. You will be either early or late, your choice, on effectiveness. You made a commitment to me. A commitment that said you would be here at 5 o'clock, and I took you at your commitment." He paused to let his words sink in. "I am not angry. I am, however, a little nervous about you because you are proving to me that your commitments are not solid. You are proving to me that you are not reliable, not predictable, therefore not trustworthy."

"I am only 2 minutes late! Are you serious?"

Tavaar waited as Adam's outburst faded in the evening air. "Only 2 minutes? If you are that sloppy with time what else are you sloppy with?"

"Umph?" Adam was in a mental state of shock, reeling at what he saw as Tavaar's complete lack of sympathy. It was like he was on the highway doing 70 and across the lanes he saw an SUV begin to roll. It momentarily interrupted his mind but was happening so fast the only thing he could do was to maintain his current speed and direction despite his desire to witness the accident.

"Adam, before I leave I want you to contemplate something and truly choose for yourself what level you are going to play at. I want you to recall the last Olympics and remember any one of the gold medal winners."

"OK, Michael Johnson."

"What did his medal do for him?"

"He made tons of money and Nike even named a pair of gold sneakers after him."

"That's right. And I suspect he gained standing among his friends as well. Another question: who won the silver medal?"

"Uh, I have no idea," shrugged Adam.

"How much money do you think he made from the fame and fortune of being in second place?"

"Not much, I don't know or even remember who he is," Adam flatly stated, his voice that of an errant schoolboy who understands the teacher's point.

Tavaar nodded. "Yes, you see, don't you? Well, seeing is not enough, Adam. Here is something I want you to think about while I am walking away."

Adam just watched the older man.

"By how much time did Michael Johnson win? How much do most Olympic athletes win by?" Tavaar held up his hand, index finger and thumb almost touching.

Adam sighed. "Fractions of a second," he said, nodding and remembering the meaty hands of his football coach from years before.

"Fractions. They pay attention to the small. They believe everything counts and it's the minuscule differences that pay off exponentially. A hundredth of a second is best in the world and your face on a cereal box, if that's the success you aim for. Millions of dollars. So what level are you playing at Adam? Have you figured out the game you're in?"

With that Tavaar walked off. Over his shoulder, he called out, "Be early next week or this adventure will cease."

The fifth meeting "Clearly on the path"

Adam arrived early the following week; it seemed as if he had spent the days in between watching every second, absorbing time itself. He had taken Tavaar very seriously, and had also decided to hold Tavaar to the same rigorous accountability. Seated with a beer, he watched as the minutes approached 5 o'clock.

Two minutes to go and no Tavaar. He began again to wonder if this guy was a crock. Who did he think he was to lecture on time if he was not committed to walking his talk?

One minute. Adam knew Tavaar was always there at 5, but this time Adam began to worry if he was going to show up at all. Maybe he feared that Tavaar was not up for working with someone like him.

Twenty seconds later, in walks Tavaar.

"Hello, Adam, it's nice to see you here early," he said as he winked, a warm smile playing on his features. "I can see by your words and actions that you have committed yourself to creating a new outcome. This will not be an easy transformation as nothing of value is. Time is not small, and value is always earned. I want to forewarn you though, that this is a process. There will be times you will wonder why you are sitting here and guessing at what value you are getting out of these interactions with me. It is when you doubt that you must re-anchor yourself in your faith."

He paused, and Adam thought vaguely about the sound of Tavaar's voice, the feel of it as it filled the space around them without the older man speaking particularly loud. Tavaar continued.

"It is faith, Adam. I can see the puzzlement in your eyes. Faith in what you are committed to creating. There will be times in our conversations and meetings that you will be uncomfortable. This is a good thing because it means you are growing. No one is good at anything the first time they try. People throw around platitudes like 'practice makes perfect,' but rarely do they understand that there is an art to life. The art of practice hones your edge."

Adam nodded, listening intently and trying to absorb his mentor's words.

"You must also be clear that I am not your friend, Adam. I do not care if you like me, and while this may sound harsh, it is not: I am not interested in coming to find you indispensable. You have plenty of friends already who do not tell you the things that you need to hear because they are more committed to you being their friend instead of being committed to your greatness. That is why I am here, Adam, to call forth your greatness. And you know that is also the reason you are here. Your greatness led me here to you."

"What do you mean?" Adam was crestfallen as he listened to the older man's seeming distance, and so this statement had caught him off balance.

"A person whose greatness was not screaming to be called forth would never have searched for me. I can see in you that throughout your entire life, you've known that there was something more but you could never figure out how to tap into it. You see others around your age making ten times the money that you do and you wonder why? Why am I not making that kind of money? What is missing in me? Why is it the good things in my life are not enough to ease this feeling? And then after a few moments of contemplation your greatness gets reburied under the shuffle and clap of life. There is always something to do, isn't there Adam? Often that something has nothing to do with calling forth your greatness. But your greatness is strong and brave within you, and that is what has you sitting here with me today. I want to acknowledge you for it." Tavaar drank from his pint.

"Uh, thank you," Adam basked in the acknowledgement. He was amazed how good he felt about himself, how quickly his feelings could shift in the presence of Tavaar.

"You are welcome. Let me tell you a story which reminds me of why I do what I do with men who do not want but who are committed. It's an old story told to me a long time ago by one of my many teachers, about why he did what he did. It is a story of six men from the East who take on an epic journey to discover paradise. They were told that paradise was over the next mountain range from their village. So the six of them set out to cross this mountain range because they wanted something better for themselves in their lives. You see, Adam, they were poor farmers much like their fathers before them and their fathers before them. That is what you were in that village at the foothills of the mountain. Being a poor farmer in that village was your sentence in life. But those six friends wanted more of an opportunity to experience their lives than what was presented to them in the village.

The six men planned, got their supplies together and began to climb. They were all very excited that they were beginning the trip to paradise to discover a fulfilled life. As they climbed the mountain they grew tired but still, they trekked upward. They knew once they climbed the mountain all new pastures would be available to them. They climbed for hours and hours; soon the hours slipped into days. They were tired, yet they continued to climb, because faith and hope pumped through their veins. When the first of the party summited the peak he gasped and whimpered at what he saw. When the others followed and viewed what the leader comprehended they too began to cry. Mountains dominated the horizon. One of the climbers sur-rendered to the impossibility of their journey, looked at his six companions and said, "It is better to be a live farmer than a dead seeker." He turned and went back to the village and the life his birth had consigned him to. The remaining five trekked on for seven years. They crossed the mountains, fought marauders, nearly lost one of their own to disease, yet they continued on their quest for paradise and a life fulfilled. At one point, they found they had crossed all the mountains they had seen from that first peak to see an immense plain stretch before them, which they traveled for months only to see another set of peaks in front of them.

Crossing those plains, one of the remaining farmers told his companions, 'I have found my paradise. I will live amongst these plains people and herd horses.' The others rejoiced that their friend found paradise amongst the horse people, but the four remaining decided to continue their quest for paradise. In the next part of their journey they climbed heavily wooded mountains in which they discovered people who made their living by lumbering. One of the four saw the great wooden houses and the fine wooden carvings and decided that now he had found his paradise and would stay amongst these woods people to live a fulfilled life. His three friends were happy for their companion but they decided to continue their quest. Finally they climbed the last set of peaks, weakened, beaten and bruised from the journey but now filled with the inner strength of seeking paradise and knowing that their friends had made their own."

Tavaar took a moment to gaze at Adam's enraptured face. He was giving Tavaar his full attention and Tavaar was pleased.

"So, Adam, they came upon this most idyllic valley, with waterfalls, pleasant weather, fertile farmlands and beautiful people. Paradise, the place to live a fulfilled life. They laughed and sung. It was the most momentous time of their lives. Two of the companions went bounding down the hill. The third looked at them and smiled lovingly at the thought that they had discovered paradise. The third also knew he had discovered paradise. The two running companions looked back and shouted 'we have discovered paradise!' 'I know!' the third shouted. 'Why aren't you coming down with us into this valley of untold paradise!' 'Because I am needed elsewhere.' 'What!' they shouted. And with tears running down his face he said, 'those that we left so many years ago need a light to show them the way. They need proof. For someone to show them the way and that this place is possible.' 'Oh, my friend,' they cried. 'They will not believe you. They will scorn you. Most do not want to endure what we have to be in a place like this. They are complacent to live their small lives, and they will revile you because you will be an example of something more that they yearn to be yet despise when they see it.' 'I know,' the would-be guide said, and he looked at his friends, his fellow seekers, with love and tears rolling down his face. 'I know my friends.' With radiance he said 'But not all of them will. There will be a few that understand and it is for those few that I am going back.'"

Tavaar was silent for a moment, his eyes a reflection of the story he was recounting. "To misquote T.S. Elliot, 'it is the 'few' that matter, not the masses of people who live in quiet desperation'. When you threw that punch at me I understood what was throwing it, for I at one time felt much the same way that you do. It's just that my journey began when I was much younger. When I told you that I was not there accidentally I wondered if the hint would have wormed its way to your greatness to ignite that curiosity and I am happy that it has."

Tavaar leaned back in his chair and sipped his Guinness. In his mind's eye Tavaar acknowledged to himself that the age-old cycle had begun once more, and that perhaps this would be his last experience of the cycle. "Do you have any questions, epiphanies or insights?"

"No," Adam shook his head. He was trying to process what this story that Tavaar shared with him meant and how it applied to his life. He had no idea how the hell this was going to help him develop his business like Brian Craig's, but he was willing to continue his commitment to the journey he was on as he somehow knew it would lead him to a better place – his paradise.

"I will see you early next week."

"Early next week?" Adam inquired.

"Before 5 o'clock."

"Yes, see you then, Tavaar."

Chapter 11

The muscle of will

Adam had come to understand the rarity of being on time, and so he made sure that his day was structured to allow him ample time to be early for his meeting with Tavaar at the tavern. When Adam opened the door to the tavern he saw Tavaar in his usual place sipping a Guinness. Before Adam could say hello Tavaar spoke:

"Adam, it looks like you lifted weights back in the day," Tavaar quipped as he leaned on the bar.

"Yeah, I did," Adam smiled as he flexed his arm and felt the hardness of his muscle.

"Why did you lift weights?"

"To get in shape." Adam answered, "To be strong."

"So at one time you were very strong?"

"Still am!" Adam looked at Tavaar and puffed up his chest.

"So what did you bench?"

"395," Adam stated with a slight nod of surety.

"Hmm, that is a lot of weight! Could you lift that kind of weight today?" inquired Tavaar. Adam knew that Tavaar was trying to teach him some sort of lesson but he could not grasp yet where he was going.

"No." Adam sighed. "I'd sure like to, but I'm afraid that just isn't gonna happen."

"Why not?"

"Because I haven't trained like that in a long time – in fact, most of my training these days is focused on eating!" laughed Adam as he patted his belly.

"So how were you able to lift that kind of weight in the past?" Tavaar raised his eyebrows inquisitively.

"I practiced at it. I was lifting consistently."

"So as you regularly lifted, your muscles grew and became stronger."

"Well, sure. That's the way it works."

"But if you went today to the gym you would not be able to lift that kind of weight?" Tavaar continued as if he were cross-examining a witness.

"That's right, I am out of practice."

"Interesting," nodded Tavaar as if he had heard an answer to the enigma Adam was trying to decipher.

"Why interesting?"

"Well, you had the muscles and then you lost them. Many never develop those kind of muscles so they never understand what it is like to have lost them. But I also think you understand that if you want to lift heavy weights you need to train your muscles to be able to perform, right?"

"Yeah, so…" Adam's face looked like he wanted to say "duh" to Tavaar but he knew better.

"A little surly today, aren't we… I want to speak with you today about a muscle that will accomplish more than all of your physical muscles put together. It is a muscle that if not exercised will atrophy. Do you know which muscle I am talking about?"

"No," Adam muttered as he shook his head.

"It's the muscle that most people ignore. It is the muscle that people do not like talking about, yet many people brag that they have a strong one. Few on this planet have one that has been well trained. Most people even avoid it when they speak."

"What do you mean, Tavaar?"

"It is the muscle of will."

Adam patted his own body, as if looking for this missing muscle. "The muscle of will?" he echoed.

"Most of our language is littered with escape clauses. The best way for me to illustrate this is to show you. Have you ever been invited to a party that you don't really want to go to but don't want to tell your friend that you do not want to go?"

"Who hasn't?" Adam grinned and rolled his eyes.

"So what do you normally tell them? Perhaps you say, I would like to go…"

Adam chimed in, "Or I will try to go. Sometimes I tell them it would be great to go but I need to check with my wife. That sort of thing."

"That's the spirit, Adam. Perhaps you even say 'maybe', 'right', or even just nod your head and say 'hmph'. Often you know full well that you will never attend your friend's party. But you lie to their face and tell them you might attend because you do not want to hurt their feelings by saying no. Unfortunately, each time you do this you sell out the power of your word to make them feel good temporarily."

"What do you mean when you say 'the power of my word' and how does that have anything to do with will?"

"Each time you give yourself the option of getting out of something with the loopholes of your language, your will listens. Your will begins to learn not to take you seriously. You begin to condition yourself to believe that it does not matter what you say. Each time your will weakens, your relationship to yourself begins to falter. The hardest thing that I had to do in all my years of teaching was to get people to believe in themselves, and that belief is founded in doing what you say. The funny thing, Adam, is that most people don't really believe what they say because they have years of practice saying 'maybe' or 'I'll try.' Rarely do they say 'I will.'"

"I don't understand, Tavaar." Adam pushed back from the bar and shifted uncomfortably on his stool, then took a drink from his beer.

" Adam, it's about cultivating belief in yourself. Most people have weak wills because they do not practice strengthening them. Just like when you lifted weights consistently in the past, your muscles grew stronger because you trained them. When we do what we say, we are engaged in an exercise in strengthening the will. Like any muscle the more that it is used the stronger it becomes."

Chapter 12

Messes we keep to suppress our greatness

The week flew by in Adam's mind. The only thing he thought of was having a beer with this man who seemed so alive, vibrant, successful and peaceful.

He rushed to the Landmark Tavern and eagerly awaited the arrival of Tavaar. The gray-haired man walked in. There was a timeless quality to his face, Adam noticed once again, lines devoid of years.

"Adam," he said, as if the two were picking up a conversation they had left off moments before, "you have already traveled far down the path, though you may not recognize it. Simply being here, despite whatever may be going on in your life, is a major victory. It tells me something about you."

"Thank you," beamed Adam.

Tavaar firmly continued, "I want you to write down the following phrase verbatim." There was a measured pace and intensity to his words, as if he believed his coming statement had the power to transform a man.

"Okay, shoot." But Adam did not move to write anything.

Tavaar sighed and shook his head, surprised at his student's ineptness. "Did you forget your notebook?" Tavaar cocked an eyebrow. "How do you plan to lock down the ideas and concepts that I share with you? Am I to guess that you are simply going to keep the knowledge that I share in your head?" Tavaar spoke with a look of shock, as if Adam were pouring Dom Perignon into plastic cups.

"Well, I have an iron trap memory and that is where I keep most of my stuff. I rarely write anything down. I am sharp, ya know! My notebook is for show." Adam tilted his head, winked and pointed at his mentor.

"Adam, you do have promise kid. I've told you that there is greatness within you. But your head is a scary place and you should not travel there alone. You have had stuff drifting inside you for over 30 years. Some of it is good, I'm certain, but a man's mind is never pure. There are other things within you, some creepy thoughts and concepts that slither about unchecked. The human head, be it a trap or a sieve, is the worst place for anything to exist. My rule of thumb is if it is in your head it does not exist. It does not hold space or time. Once something is committed to paper the exact idea holds space and time until it is destroyed. But the crap in your head is shifting, dissolving and rearranging all of the time. Your memory fades and often gets jumbled. Do not allow the gems that I share with you to fall into the tar pit of your mind."

"But I am smarter than most people you know!" Adam replied a little defensively.

"Yes, I know. It's your smartness that has gotten you exactly where you are now. If you want more of what you already have now, keep doing what you have always done. It works in getting you what you already have. If you want something new, listen and write it down!"

Adam looked at his feet and mumbled, "Okay."

Adam grabbed a pen from the inside of his coat and flipped over a bar coaster.

"Write this down" Tavaar said, "You are the sun and whatever you shall shine upon shall grow. Let me repeat, "You are the sun and whatever you shall shine upon shall grow. In simple English whatever you pay attention to you get more of."

"What does that mean Tavaar?"

"I imagine that you have houseplants. Have you ever noticed how all those houseplants lean towards the windows?" Adam nodded. "They grow towards the sun. Your attention is as powerful as the sun, and whatever you shall shine upon shall grow. Attention is the essence of life as well as its creation. The fastest way to kill a plant is to put it in the closet. Attention creates and attention can also destroy. The lack of attention also creates and destroys. We need to be very mindful of what we give our attention to as there are serious consequences if we do not."

"That seems obvious."

"Obvious? Perhaps, but rarely is it foremost in a man's mind. Rarely does it become second nature. Think about a trip to the dentist. He looks at your teeth and tells you if you don't pay attention to your teeth, you will develop some serious problems. Take good care of them – i.e. give them attention – they will serve you for your entire life. Hopefully, what I've just said helps to drive home what you seem to think is obvious. Your attention is very powerful." Tavaar paused to drink. "What many people do not notice, or do not stop to notice, is that their attention is scattered over many things and many places. They are unfocused and randomly spread their attention over a myriad of tasks, people, goals and places. They practice the model of the over-scheduled child, rushing about from one thing to the next, believing they live well-rounded lives, when in reality they scarcely live at all. Scattered attention produces scattered results. Random attention produces random results. I suppose there is nothing wrong with random attention if what you are committed to is getting random results. But is that a model for a good life? Let's think about this for a moment: what is the probability that random results will produce a business or a life lived by design? Randomness is anathema to design. Attention, like will, is a muscle and as with all muscles it can be strengthened. Unfortunately, most people do not know how to strengthen the muscle of attention. Very soon you will, Adam. But before we can strengthen this muscle of attention we need to create the space to do it."

"What do you mean by creating space, Tavaar?"

"Good question, son. Let me tell you a little story to prove the point of the power of space. What is your favorite spectator sport?"

"Football."

"What team do you like the best?"

"The New England Patriots."

"Imagine you get great tickets to see the Patriots play. You're sitting on the 50-yard line and you arrive to the game just before kickoff. The game starts but from your great seats you notice that something's a little strange. You notice that the playing field is a mess – it has pickup trucks parked on it, a couple of garbage cans, even an old laundry machine. What's really strange about this is that the players don't seem to notice, or at least to care that these messes cluttering their field. These are highly trained professional athletes running at full speed and every now and then they smash head-on into a parked pickup or garbage can. After they shake off the impact they simply get up and keep playing football. Of course you notice this is very odd, you are an outside observer. But they continue to play full-bore with these obstacles on their field, as though it is normal. Something becomes blatantly obvious to you: for these athletes to truly perform at their highest level they need a clear field to play their game. The messes on this field interfere with the execution of their game. So even for the greatest athletes, if their field is marred by disruptions to its space, their performance will suffer. Likewise, for you to begin to perform in your business and your life, you need a clear field to play on. A clear playing field allows your greatest gifts and talents to flourish."

"That makes sense. I can see that in order to truly excel in your sport you need a clear field to perform on. But what else do you mean by a mess? Pickups on a football field are pretty obvious obstacles, but how does this relate to the way I do business?"

"A mess is something that takes your attention. I didn't say the players totally fail to see the obstacles, they do nothing about them. A mess is something that you know you should take care of but you just don't seem to have the time or desire to do anything about it. You see, Adam, we all have a limited quantity of attention and it is easily taken or overwhelmed. Imagine you are going to give the Best Man's speech at your friend's wedding and you are trying to come up with something witty to say. Your mind is churning these ideas over and over and you realize that you have to get in your car and get to the event. You've been having fun with creating the speech but you realize that you cannot find your keys. Suddenly all of the speech disappears and you begin to desperately hunt for your missing set of keys. A mess has suddenly oozed into your world. Your attention is hijacked, now 100% focused on finding the keys instead of crafting the speech to acknowledge your friend. Imagine if you lost your keys every day, how frustrating that would be to you and how disrupting and inefficient your day would be if you constantly had to hunt frantically for those keys?"

"So not being able to find my keys would be considered a mess?"

"Yes, because it hijacks your mind. When it hijacks your mind, you can't think or create anything else except 'find the keys.' And those three words are rarely a simple conversation you have with yourself. When someone loses their keys their internal dialogue is usually shouting at them, 'You are an idiot, how the hell did you lose your keys, why are you always so stupid, why does my wife always try to undermine me by hiding my keys."

Adam laughed and said, "Your wife does that to you too?"

"No," Tavaar said with a taint of seriousness. "She does not. But do you understand what I mean. A mess often causes more problems and diversions than we think. It interferes with our field of play. Let me give you a more insidious example."

Adam lifted his eyebrows in response.

"Where do you park your car when you come home?"

"In the garage," Adam flipped nonchalantly.

"Good, just like most people. When you go to work in the morning, you go into the garage and hop in the car. Right?"

"Yep."

"Now, I am not saying that *you* do this but when many people walk into their garages and survey its contents, they mumble to themselves 'Man this place is a mess. I have got to clean and organize this junk pile but I just don't have the time.' People have these internal conversations everyday for years and still the garage is not clean. The messy garage actually becomes an enforcer of a negative self-image. It becomes a structure that reinforces the illusion of smallness. They have just put another deposit into the proverbial negative jar, one more way in which they find themselves lacking."

"Yeah, I suppose so. ."

"But every day, they jump into their car, which is usually a mess as well, and that's another deposit into the negative jar. They get to the office with papers flung everywhere, again, another deposit. So even before they start working, they have multiple deposits into that jar. Are they setting themselves up for high performance?"

"No, probably not."

"So Adam, I think I've been clear!"

"Yes."

"Then consider this, what are your biggest messes? Keep in mind, a mess can be physical, mental, financial, and spiritual or relational. It is anything that is hijacking your attention. A pile of garbage or a 30-pound spare tire around your waist. A mess is that proverbial pickup truck on the fifty-yard line."

"I see your point. You're saying that I live in a trap set by the messes that I have not dealt with, and they prevent me from reaching my potential in my business and life."

"Exactly, Adam. Traps indeed. The litter and detritus of your life catches your attention and structures your smallness, not your greatness."

"I can see this with some things, but come on, my messy car is a structure for my smallness? How's that? Who cares about my car?"

"Everything we see, we remember, Adam. You said so yourself. Everything we see tells us something – it sends us a signal. A messy car tells you something every time you see it. What could a messy car be communicating to you?"

"Really Tavaar, a car doesn't talk to you."

"No shit. Don't be so dense. What does a car full of empty coffee cups piled up on the floor say about the owner?"

"He likes coffee, but he doesn't care about the car. Maybe he is sloppy or low-class, or maybe he doesn't have the time to clean it."

"Now think of this, every time he gets behind the wheel that message is relayed to him. If a person gets a certain message enough times they begin to believe it. It begins to fill their attention and from what I said earlier, whatever you give your attention to you get more of. And that just begs an age-old question: is what I am paying attention to worth my attention? Do I really want more of this?"

Adam blurted out, "Can't you just ignore the messy car and keep focused on what you want."

"An advanced mind maybe, but Adam, you are not there yet so go and clean you car!" laughed Tavaar. "Get out of here and begin to clear your playing field so you can perform at your highest level."

Adam left the tavern and began to ponder what his messes were. He knew his office and garage were in semi-shambles. He also patted his stomach and noticed his physical mess of a gut. 'Hmm' he thought to himself 'I have some work to do.'

Chapter 13

Wisdom at the bottom of a glass

Much to Adam's surprise Tavaar did not order his usual Guinness. "Barkeep, pour my friend," Tavaar requested, "some of your house whiskey. As a matter of fact make that two, and we'll have those both straight up in a short glass."

"Why, Tavaar," Adam raised his eyebrow as well as the pitch of his voice, "a change in your usual Guinness? What's with that?"

"As in all things that I do, it is for a purpose. And that purpose is to introduce you to the vividness of existence."

"Well I appreciate that. Sounds intriguing."

"Adam, I have an interesting lesson for you today, in the most unlikely place, this common drinking establishment." Tavaar raised his glass and toasted the entire bar. "Our teachers are all around us and the Universe wants us to fulfill our highest calling. But oftentimes we are too asleep to see all those helpful hands that are extended to us. Our teacher today will be Mr. Jack Daniels. I know he's an old friend of yours – you have much to thank him for." Tavaar extended his glass towards Adam and winked.

"That's not funny, Tavaar."

"Oh, it is funny, Adam. If you did not have those drinks you would have never met me. And if you had never met me your path would be unchanged. So knock back your whiskey and tell me what you taste."

Adam drank the shot of whiskey, shook his head and spoke to Tavaar. "Well the taste is unique. It slightly burns and has a bit of a bite."

"That wasn't all that descriptive, but it'll do. Tell me, if you have five more of those what would happen to you?"

"Five for me? Probably not much." Adam says with a grin.

"Fair enough. You're a big boy. Let's make that 10."

"Ten, I would be pretty drunk."

"You sure would."

Tavaar tipped his glass to Adam with a twinkle in his eye and said "Bottoms up my friend," finishing off the rest of his own whiskey.

Tavaar leaned over the bar and called out, "Barkeep, my friend and I would like Makers Mark whiskey. Once again put it in a short glass but this time with ice." They waited while the bartender poured their drinks. "Adam, when you get it, taste it and tell me about it."

This time Adam did not down the whiskey in a single gulp. "That's smooth and nice. It's palatable but doesn't burn. Nice texture; definitely a sipping whiskey."

"Now if you had 10 of these what would happen?"

"I would be pretty drunk."

"Sure you would. Notice that the taste is different. So would you choose this one over the first?

"Yes, if I wanted a sipping whiskey."

"Now could you do shots of Makers Mark?"

"Sure I could, but that doesn't seem right."

"Interesting distinction, Adam. Notice that drinking both brands, the outcome is the same, you still get drunk. But the journey to getting drunk is a little different.

"Okay I see that, but I don't know what you're getting at."

"You will, don't worry. But first, let's take a few moments here to enjoy this sipping whiskey before our next lesson."

Adam and Tavaar pushed back from the bar almost simultaneously, then looked at their glasses, noticing the honey-amber color, the tinkle of the ice as they swirled the liquid, sipped and sighed. Each thinking to themselves how good life is and how wonderful it is to be in the company of fine men.

"This would be a fine whiskey to have a great cigar with," Adam stated wistfully.

"Wish that we had them. But let's continue the lesson. Barkeep, pour my friend and I two Budweisers'. I think I'd be safe in betting you it that tastes like beer."

"Honestly, I think that depends on what you think beer should taste like."

"Hmm, touché. But let's put aside the comparative merits for a moment. If you drank 10 of those what would happen?"

"I would be pretty drunk."

"Of course you would be. This is a great analogy to life. No matter what you are drinking if you have 10 drinks you will be drunk. Whether it's whiskey, wine, tequila or beer, the outcome is the same. You get drunk. So what matters here is what you actually choose to drink and the reason you choose it. It's your personal choice. It is the same with life. The outcome is always the same with you, your neighbors or a stranger on the other side of the world. You die. So what really matters is how you choose to live. Unfortunately, most people are not conscious enough to choose how they live. They drink Firebird instead of Makers Mark or Boones Farm instead of the finest wine. The outcome is all the same. It is your choice that makes all of the difference. The choices of being poor are just as easy to make as the choices of being wealthy. Many people argue with me and say people do not choose to be poor or that people do not choose to be wealthy, it's just what they end up as. But while these may be unconscious choices, they are choices nonetheless. The choices we do not make are just as powerful as the choices that we do make. Whether you are rich or poor, happy or sad, in a great relationship or in a poor relationship, they are all the results of the choices you have made or the choices that you failed to make. So the gist of this conversation is to be aware of what you are choosing. Be aware of what you are giving your attention to because you're the sun and whatever you shall shine upon shall grow."

"So my life is about what I choose to drink?" inquired Adam.

"Proverbially speaking, yes, Adam. Now go home and until we meet again be conscious of your choices and why you are making them."

Chapter 14

Metabolizing the booze

After Adam left the bar Tavaar's words began to sink into his head. He knew intellectually that he was going to die, but it wasn't something that he ever really thought about. But Tavaar had put it in a way that made him actually consider its meaning.

What if he were right, Adam thought. What if it did not really matter what you did but only that you chose what you did. The outcome was the same for everyone on the planet but power could come from choosing how you're going to live and how to conduct your business.

Adam began to ponder all the things that he did in his life. He did a lot of what he was supposed to do or mimicked what everyone else was doing. He began to feel that much of his life happened unconsciously. He had spent his life just going along, not really choosing or even considering that he had choices to make. I do what everyone expected me to do. He remembered the words of his friend, who had just not been someone who would get divorced, and Adam realized that his own dissatisfaction with his life had come out of being stuck in expectations that he had not chosen.

'With full choice would I pick my career?' he asked himself. 'Maybe. But would I conduct it a little differently?'

He at first thought no, but then he realized that was a lie; he would conduct it exponentially differently. He thought of Herb Fay and his constant quest for more, the bigger watch, the bigger house, the hotter wife, a never-ending, never-fulfilling cycle.

He wouldn't stop his business. Tavaar's words ran through his head. 'The outcome is that I am drunk no matter what I choose to drink. So then the power comes in what you are choosing and the reason why you choose what you choose is because you chose it.' Adam laughed to himself at that thought. He wondered if he could say that tongue twister 3 times fast.

Adam's mind began to pick up speed as he walked down the street towards his neighborhood. He began to examine this concept of choice. What did it mean to him? He thought of Herb and his $25,000 watch and his constant nattering about how it commands respect. Adam thought that was a little weird. Does a watch really command respect? As Adam thought he began to see the reason why Herb did the things he did. It was to impress others. He was projecting his self-importance upon other people. But why would anyone need to impress other people? 'Tiger Woods is a great golfer but he does not seem to be projecting his greatness on others. He just is great. He doesn't need to tell anyone or impress anyone. He simply plays great golf.'

In that moment Adam had an amazing insight. He thought to himself, 'Tiger Woods does not need to play golf. He has more than enough money to do whatever he chooses to do. Yet he continues to play golf despite having more than enough money to ensure that his future generations will never have to work. Wow! Tiger is choosing the drink of golf because the outcome is the same no matter what he chooses but he is choosing golf wholeheartedly.' Adam began to think about choosing his profession.

He found himself literally skipping down the street simply because he chose to do so and he was giddy with excitement to see Tavaar the next week, and to tell him about his epiphany.

Chapter 15

Mess of the mind

As Adam walked towards the Landmark Tavern for his weekly meeting with Shane Tavaar he reflected back on his progress and he smiled. Life seemed to be unfolding in a more favorable direction. It seemed that effortlessness was becoming part of his being. Things happened easier by simply being on time, by realizing that everything was his responsibility. When he took responsibility for things he owned the outcome. If he did not own the outcome he became a victim of circumstances and he did not like being a victim.

As Adam bounded up the steps he was excited to share his insight about Tiger Woods and drinking the game of golf.

Adam saw Tavaar in the corner when he entered, and walked over to him. The two men shook hands, and as Adam sat down, he said, "Tavaar, I think I finally understand something that you have tried to share with me."

"Really? What could that be?"

"That whole thing about choosing what kind of life you are going to drink because the outcome is the same no matter what you choose."

"Go on."

"I think I got it. Take Tiger Woods. He chooses to play golf not because he has to, but because he wants to. It's his choice."

"Nice, Adam. So how do you know that Tiger chooses to play golf?"

"Cause he doesn't need to play the game anymore. He has more than enough money to do anything that he chooses to do, yet he continues to play the game."

"Why do you think he plays?"

"Because he loves the game."

"Exactly, Adam. Do you think he would play golf even if he never made any money at it?"

"Yeah, I do."

"I think you're right. He makes a lot of money playing golf, exactly because of the commitment and love for the game that he brings to his play. Because it is not about the money. It's about his choice and his commitment to

104

the choice. Imagine, Adam, if you were to choose wholeheartedly the drink of your particular business. What would that look like to you?"

"Wow! So to make a lot of money it has to be about not caring about making a lot of money?"

"Strange, isn't it? It's about being committed to the outcome yet unattached to the result. This is not exactly the same thing, but in Plato's book The Republic, Socrates distinguishes between what he calls the art of money-making and other arts. His point is to show that, say, a doctor aims at bringing or restoring health to the patient – that's the goal of the practice of medicine and the fact that he gets paid for it is because he also is engaged in the practice of money-making. Being paid is a separate goal. But this matter of wanting an outcome without worrying excessively about the result, we can talk more about that later."

"Good, I'd like that."

"I'm more interested at the moment in returning to something we discussed a few weeks ago. Remember how we spoke about messes and how they can steal your attention."

"Yes, of course."

"I've been reflecting on our interactions and my observations of you, and today I am going to share with you your biggest mess. It's a mess that keeps most people from ever reaching the level of Tiger Woods in anything that they do. But if you choose to work on it, the Way of the Tiger is open to you.

"The way of the tiger? That sounds kinda' strange."

"Perhaps, but my words are deliberate. No doubt you know that Taoism embraces 'the way'. In fact the very meaning of the Chinese word 'tao' means 'way.' In Taoism, to give you a somewhat simple view, the way is a path that a man can follow to achieve harmony with what the Taoists call the 'ten thousand things' – basically a cipher that represents the entirety of the cosmos. Is this familiar to you?"

"Vaguely. I took an eastern philosophy class in college," said Adam. With a grin, he added, "but it's been a while."

"Indeed it has. Well, I said I'm being deliberate in choosing my words. This is what I mean by 'the way.' It's more than achieving harmony, in fact I don't really have Taoism in mind, I simply mention it to make a distinction, even though that version is related to what I have to say. 'The way' that I'm talking about is a commitment to excellence in whatever and all that you do. Where everything is taken on as a practice to hone you and whatever you choose to be. Just as in the old days when a warrior was a warrior in all that he did. Is that clear?"

"Yeah, I think so. But I have to ask, you said that what you're talking about is probably related to what you said about Taoism. I got to admit, the connection isn't jumping out at me."

"Well, think about this. The Taoist philosopher Chuang Tzu told a story about a butcher. He's exceptionally skilled, and someone asks him about his work. He says that when he first became a butcher, he had to consistently work

106

at maintaining his cleaver and knives, regularly sharpening them. But over time, as he learned his craft, the need to sharpen them diminished. His movements became more precise, the knife 'found' the joint and cut through with less effort. Through consistent attention, he became a master of his trade, by harmonizing his actions with the materials he worked on."

"Ah, I gotcha. That sounds very similar."

"It is related. But I'm talking about inhabiting a role fully, being what you are in everything you do. The distinction may be small, but it's important. In any event, my aim today is to handle the mess that prevents 'The Way' for you."

"You've definitely piqued my interest."

"For this lesson we need to make an assumption. The assumption is that an orderly business is more productive than a chaotic business; likewise an orderly mind is better than a chaotic mind. We will also need to assume that your business, as well as your life, is a direct reflection of the contents of your mind. Can you get that Adam?"

"Sure. That's pretty simple - an orderly business like McDonald's produces more and makes more money than the local yokel hamburger stand, run by a guy who doesn't think beyond the food he's making and can't figure out how to set regular rules," stated Adam.

"You're getting smarter. If we improve your mind, your business and life will also improve. Can you get that? Adam, what kind of car do you drive?"

"A Mercedes."

"That is a fine example of a German engineering. Would you say that's a pretty good car?"

"I'd say it's the best."

"Now imagine if you left your car running 24 hours a day, seven days a week, for the foreseeable future. What would happen to that finely engineered German car?"

"Eventually it would break down from wear and tear."

"Right. Even a fine car like yours, if run constantly, will begin to break down. This is a great analogy for our lives. If you want optimal performance from your car or even your body it needs time to rest and it needs maintenance. Does this make sense so far?"

"Yes, it does."

"Let me give you a real life example. Have you ever watched the TV show 'Cops?'"

"Yeah – bad boys, bad boys, they're coming for you," Adam sang.

"Yes. I never knew you had so little talent for singing" said Tavaar with a grin.

"Thanks a lot!"

"Nothing personal – you're just a bit off-key. Anyway, one day I was watching it and I saw these guys do the dumbest things as they ran from the police. I asked myself why these people would do such stupid things? They were jumping off bridges, driving their cars into telephone poles, throwing punches and, even worse, shooting at the police. It was some really stupid stuff."

"Hey, Shane, I even saw a bunch of guys drive their car off a bridge to get away from the cops."

"My first thought was that they're criminals, and of course they're stupid, but then I thought a little further. They are human beings and they start out with the same capacity as you and I, within a range, so why would they do such stupid things? It's quite simple Adam; stress makes you stupid. The more stress you are under the dumber you become! As your stress level rises, your capacity for processing thought decreases."

"Why's that, Tavaar?"

"It's all about evolution. As your fight-or-flight mechanism kicks into high gear your blood starts rushing to your extremities and a high dose of adrenaline flows through your system. This is a survival mechanism that stems from millions of years of savage circumstances that we don't encounter any more on a daily basis. Fortunately we no longer need to run from lions, tigers and bears. Instead our stress comes from deadlines, our bosses, self-imposed goals, and even our families. Most of what we deal with today acquires a higher level of thought, which is exactly what the fight-or-flight response does not produce. We don't need to fight or flee most of the time today, we need to think, yet the stress response interferes with high-level thinking. When our minds are cluttered our outcome is unclear and when our outcome is unclear we operate by default instead of by design. It is easy to get lost when we lack clarity."

"I never thought about it that way, Tavaar."

"Like I said, it's quite simple. Adam, stress makes you stupid. And stupid people make stupid choices, which always lead to painful results."

"Aren't you being a little extreme, Tavaar?"

"Perhaps, Adam, but I'm trying to teach you something. Your mind works best when it is in a relaxed state free from the clutter. Think of when you get your best ideas or greatest client insights. They often happen when you are in the shower or on vacation somewhere removed from the day-to-day stresses, clutter and noise of your life and business. Even a low level of stress muddies the mind. It makes you less efficient than you could be. You mentioned Tiger Woods. Remember how he used to play golf before he muddied the waters of his personal life? He used to play moment to moment with a clear mind; now he occurs as angry as his game suffers. I submit his mind is still muddy wether it be guilt of a lost identity. He has lost his way."

"Shane, what do you mean by a muddy mind?"

"Let me tell you a story. Presumably you've had bottled water?" inquired Tavaar.

"Yes."

"Do you have a favorite?"

"Evian, I suppose."

"Imagine that you are sleeping in your hammock in your backyard. Your water bottle is at your side. What's the name of your younger boy again?"

"Geno."

"Now imagine that for one day he is a little terror and while you sleep he decides to play a trick on Daddy by putting an inch of dirt in your water bottle and shaking it up. By chance you wake up right after he put the dirt in but you're thirsty and you take a swig of the water without really looking at it first. What does it taste like?"

"Well, dirt of course. But what's your point?"

"Bear with me. So it tastes like mud. Now imagine after the little cherub puts the dirt in a bottle and shakes it up you fall back asleep for another 40 minutes and and he is there waiting beside you to wake up. You wake up again thirsty, you see your smiling little child's face, grab your water bottle and drink the water. What does it taste like?"

"Mud, I guess."

"No. It tastes like water. The dirt has had time to settle. Once the bottle stops being shaken the dirt has time to settle to the bottom. When the bottle is agitated it is cloudy. When the dirt settles you have clarity. We often have to take time to allow the mud of the mind to settle."

"Okay, I can see that."

"When you allow the mud of the mind to settle you can see with clarity. You can freely choose your outcome. I intend to start sharing with you a toolset to create clarity for the mind. But in order to do this we need to take a trip. Meet me here next week at our regular time but bring a change of clothes. We are going to go to my cabin."

Chapter 16

The truck trip north

At 5 pm instead of Adam bounding up the stairs, he waited in front of the bar at the cross roads of Hamm and Center Street. He had brought a change of clothes and his sleeping bag. He had an interesting conversation with his wife when he told her that he was going to a sleep over party in the woods with this guy Shane Tavaar. He was surprised just how easy the conversation was and how supportive she was of his spending time with this man. She basically said that any time you spend with that man makes a difference for you and our family, so the more time you spend with him the better off we all will all be.

Tavaar pulled up in a late model pick up truck with a smile on his face.

"Get in boy and let's go for a ride."

Adam hopped in the truck as he threw his gear in the back. The truck reminded him of his father's truck and the endless times he picked Adam up at Football practice before Adam got his own car.

"This is not what I expected from you Tavaar"

"No. What did you expect?"

"I thought you would have some sort of new fancy kind of ride."

"Really? I have those as well Adam. What you just mentioned is an interesting example of expectations and the filters we use in life, how quick we are to judge things and people. It is yet another example of how that mess of your mind can interfere with your life. It can add color and flavor to things that would not be present except for the interference of your mind."

"Tavaar you make my mind sound like a bad thing. Like it is something out of control."

"It is not a bad thing. Ha, I like how you said "my" mind. It's "your" mind just like it is "your" car. You have made the distinction that it is not you? But something that is apart from "you."

"What?" Adam turned to Tavaar as he piloted the pickup down the highway towards the hills up north.

"This will be an interesting journey for you Adam. For on this simple journey you may discover a whole new you that you never met but always have known."

"Man, Tavaar you are really starting to sound like Mr. Miaggi from <u>The Karate Kid</u>."

"Who?" Shane looked at Adam quizzically as if he made some sort of arcane cultural reference.

"So tell me more about this 'my mind' concept."

"You see Adam one of mankind's greatest foibles is that we think our thoughts are true and, much worse, we think the contents of our minds are who we are. We identify with the noise going on in our heads as if it is true and our identity."

"I don't understand Tavaar."

"I know. Let me try to deepen your understanding. First let's talk about "my".

"Ok."

"**My** connotes ownership right? My car, my house, my jeans, my coffee. Would you agree?"

"Yes."

"Now what are some of the principles of ownership or how do we know that we own something?"

"We get to use it."

"Right, so like your car you turn the ignition and it goes. You know how to use it and it performs a particular function. Your car transports you places. It is predictable."

"Relatively predictable as long as you maintain it."

"Got that. If you maintain something, it also means that you are responsible for it."

"Ok", Adam nodded along.

"Let me ask you a few more questions about this car that you "own".

"Go ahead."

"Where is it right now?"

"In my driveway."

"Excellent. Since you own the car you have put it in your driveway and you can expect it will stay right where you left it. Correct?"

Adam nodded.

"Where will your car be at 4 in the morning tomorrow?"

"In the drive way."

"How about at 10am tomorrow morning?"

"Still in the drive way."

"Since you own it, there is a level of predictability as well as a high probability of function. In other words, whenever you are ready to use it for its purpose, it will function properly. It will get you where you need to go."

"Right."

"So some of the things we have established with ownership is predictability of place and function. We know where our car is and it will perform its function. But obviously your car is not a part of you."

"What do you mean by 'not part of me'?"

"Well, you would still exist without your car right?"

"Obviously."

"Now let's restate the principles of ownership, you know where it is and what it does or what it will do."

"OK"

"Let's bring ownership of your mind to the forefront of this conversation."

"Ok"

"What will you be thinking about 15 minutes from now?"

"I don't know."

"How will you be feeling 15 minutes from now?"

"I don't know."

"What will you be thinking about 2 days from now?"

"I have no idea."

"Where will your car be?"

"In the driveway."

"How will you be feeling 2 days from now?"

"I do not know."

"Will your car work 2 days from now?"

"Most likely."

"Interesting conversation isn't it Adam? Do you really own your mind? Is your mind really you?"

"Yes, Yes, of course it is me", Adam stammered. His head was beginning to spin slightly. He was a little uncomfortable with this conversation. "Of course I am what I think about, aren't I? If I can't own my mind or I'm not my mind then who am I? Who's mind is it?"

"Of course you are the contents of your mind Adam. Maybe your thoughts are true and real but for play sake let's go a little further with this conversation." Tavaar smiled wryly with the look of a professor who has just steered a student into a logic trap.

Adam was beginning to regret that he took this trip with this strange man. He was in a capsule that he could not escape from. He was being forced to confront something that he sort of knew but always feared and wasn't quite sure if he was ready for.

"So who are you Adam?"

"I am me. I am Adam Arbor."

"Are you really? Are you just a mere name, a symbol, a collection of letters and words?"

"No, I am more than that."

"Yes you are Adam, but first let's find out what you are not."

"Ok." Adam said with a level of dread because he knew under his skin that this was going to hurt in some way. He got a sense that things would never quite be the same after this little interchange.

"Adam, let me see your watch. I want you to look at it. Look at it as if this were the first time you ever saw it. Give it your complete attention."

"Ok"

"Now that you are observing it, is that watch you?"

"No."

"Do you own that watch?"

"No."

"Can you exist without your watch? Do you notice an existence without your watch?"

"Yes of course."

"So since you can observe your watch, your watch cannot be you right? To observe anything requires an observer. Or in simple English a subject and an object."

"Ok."

"Now Adam, observe the shirt you have on. Since you can observe your shirt then your shirt cannot be you, right?"

"Right."

"So without your shirt you would still be you right?"

"Yes."

"Now Adam, look at your arm. Observe your arm. Imagine you are a thief in Saudi Arabia who has been caught stealing from the market and while facing Arab justice you lose your arm. Without your arm would you be you?"

"Yes."

"So since you can observe your arm, your arm cannot be you right? For anything that you can observe cannot be you."

"Ok I am getting it Tavaar."

"Now let's make this conversation even more interesting. Adam I want to bring your attention inward to the contents of your mind. Observe your thoughts. What you are thinking about? Are you observing your thoughts Adam?"

"Yes I am."

"What are you thinking about?"

"How long is this ride going to be? Where is he going with this?"

"Great! So if you can observe your thoughts Adam, much like you can observe your watch, your shirt, or your arm. You cannot be your mind, so who are you Adam? If anything you can observe cannot be you, then who are you Adam?"

"I am me?"

"And who is that? Remember anything you can observe cannot be you."

"My God Tavaar who am I if I am not the contents of my mind?"

"That is a great inquiry Adam. In time you will discover who you are, perhaps by the end of our journey together." Tavaar smiled at Adam as he pulled off the road to a long and windy driveway. They had arrived at Tavaar's cabin in the woods.

Chapter 17

A trip to the woods

Tavaar's cabin was rustic, yet modern at the same time. The trees framed his cabin in a canopy of green. The smell of pine clutched the ground in a blanket. It was a peaceful place. A large fieldstone fireplace dominated the cabin from the outside and a wrap-around porch hugged each wall. It looked like it could have been owned by a frontiersman a hundred years ago. As they got out of the truck and approached the cabin it seemed that Tavaar's footsteps got lighter. His face lit up. It was clear, he enjoyed it here.

"Adam, isn't the air refreshing? Can you taste the pine?" Tavaar continued, not giving Adam time to answer. "I chose this place because of the isolation, the views and the trees. It's a place to come and unplug from the city. Many a man gets caught up in the trials and tribulations of the city and forgets his roots. We come from nature. There is a reason why they call it Mother Nature. I love the city, it was created by man for men. That's why it is so important to come to nature created by the creator for the sheer enjoyment of the creator. It is said that if you truly listen to nature, you can hear the voice of God. It is a voice that soothes and calms. It's a voice that brings clarity to the mind. Can you hear it Adam?"

"Can I hear what Tavaar?"

"The sound that is always there, Adam."

"Tavaar, can we get the stuff out of the truck before you start getting all woo hoo on me again?" Adam kids.

"Grasshopper the world is your dojo, and often times the lessons that are taught are not convenient to the walls of the classroom. If you are open to it, the world and every experience is your teacher. Unfortunately, your mind is often so polluted and corrupted, it doesn't warrant the lessons that are constantly being taught to you. If you actually opened your mind you wouldn't be in the situation that you're currently in. You would have all that you desired, if you would just listen. The teachers have always been there, and they will always be there pointing to the way. The challenge lies in that the mind is often not where the body is."

"Tavaar what do you mean that the mind is not where the body is? My mind is wherever I am. Sometimes I don't want my mind to be where I am actually." Adam looked at Tavaar and pondered his mind.

"Adam, unfortunately, that is not true. Most of the time you are nowhere near where your mind is. Although your body may occupy a certain space your mind is often years forward or years in the past. That is the essence of why so many people suffer, why so many are not happy. A major cause is that they don't hear the sound that's always there. Your mind is always processing information. How this ties into that, how this could affect that, why they should do this, and who should do that, where should this be and on and on.

125

This is sad. This is not good. It's a constant chatter. Very rarely is someone present to the beauty and the glory of life. For when you are present to hear the voice of the sound that is always there."

"When are we going to eat?" Adam tapped his less ample belly.

"See that is a perfect example." Tavvar pointed at Adam's belly. "Instead of listening to what I am saying and processing it you are listening to your stomach. Yet again the opportunity for you to go somewhere else other than where you are right now materializes. It amazes me sometimes that I have the patience to deal with you! May my teacher be blessed for his patience with me. But that is what you are, a grasshopper and your mind is just about as green."

"Well, let's eat now since your mind is so distracted. Perhaps some food will calm the attack, so that I can share with you the purpose of why we came to this beautiful place in the woods." Tavaar turned his head to survey the trees and dug his hand into the earth and let the soil crumble between his fingers.

"Tavaar, what were you saying about the sound that's always there?"

"Oh you are interested now? So grasshopper, how can there always be a sound? How can there be a sound even when there is silence? Is not the definition of silence, no sound? So how can there be a sound that is always there?" Tavaar crossed his arms and waited for a response.

"I don't know" Adam shrugged is shoulders and looked to Tavaar "can you tell me more about it?"

"Of course I can tell you more about it. Are you done eating yet? I can see by that look on your face that you are semi-full. If you would like to hear the sound that is always there I need to take you through a quick exercise. Are you up for it?"

"Sure."

"Let me share with you a little bit about the sound that is always there." Tavaar smiled and his face relaxed as his body centered itself. He pointed to a chair on his porch and said: "Take a seat on this chair, on my porch and I just want you to sit and listen. I will share with you, the concept of the sound that is always there. So sit in an upright yet relaxed position."

The pine trees swayed in the gentle breeze, the squirrels continued their never ending quest for finding lost nuts. Two men sat on a porch in silence.

Chapter 18

Stillness - settling the mud

"That is right Adam, sit tall and proud. Imagine you are a king reviewing your troops you would sit a certain way. You would sit regally."

"Like this?" Adam sat like his mom would be proud of him. Back straight, legs with a nice 90° bend at the knee and hands open palms down on the thighs.

"Very good. Now as you are sitting there let me re-visit a few things I have shared with you over the last few months and in our recent trip up here. Hopefully I have established with you that space is what makes things usable. Your house is functional, not because of the furniture in it, but the space around the furniture. The emptiness, if you will."

"Yeah I remember, it's the space in my coffee cup which makes my coffee cup usable."

"Very good."

"When rooms become cluttered, their functionality declines. Likewise, if a business gets cluttered it becomes more difficult to conduct business. If you were an auto mechanic and you never put your tools back in the same place you may find that you have a tendency to do more finding than fixing, which affects your bottom line."

"Ok, I can see that."

"Messes are an example of things that create clutter in the living room of the mind. As you noticed when you cleaned up your messes you began to create more mental space. You may be wondering why it's important to create mental space."

"Yes I am."

"Remember the quote 'You are the sun and whatever you shall shine upon shall grow'?"

Adam nodded his head.

"Many people waste their attention by continually grappling with messes and the after effects of a mess. They are not clear that their attention is being absorbed by a mess which we will consider a default or conscious manifestation. Or if the mind is simply cluttered with chatter and distractions of the day, it cannot produce on the level it was built for. Most people do not realize that their attention is absorbed every day by minor problems and minor people, hence why they live relatively common, mediocre lives. What I am about to share with you is a tool to help you clarify your attention."

"What are you saying Shane? Are you saying that most of my success or lack of success in some areas is because I wasn't paying attention?"

"Unfortunately, yes. It is a simply brilliant statement of whatever you pay attention to, you get more of. Whatever you have in life is the result of your attention and whatever you lack is the result of your inattention. Adam, the challenge is that no one has ever taught you a way to cultivate your attention and your power of will. Yet it is these two concepts which create everything. So now you are about to learn."

"I'm excited!"

"You should be, but I want to remind you, that this is a process and it will take time and much practice for you to notice the subtle differences in the quality of mind."

"Ok."

"So let's get back to it. Bring your attention to your body. Notice what it feels like to have a body. Notice the distinction between you and the chair that you are sitting in. Become aware of the subtle ebb and flow of air against any exposed skin. Feel yourself beginning to relax. Allow each breath you take to bring you deeper. One of the fastest ways to draw your attention inward is to focus on the trail of your breath. That's it Adam, feel yourself getting deeper and deeper. Realize that there is nowhere to go, just everywhere to be. Allow yourself to luxuriate in the moment of now."

Adam felt his entire body relaxing, he didn't know why but he had done this type of relaxation exercise before. He could actually feel his mind begin to settle, although it did keep bouncing around from things he had to do at work, to wondering what his wife was doing, to the sound of Tavaar's voice.

Tavaar continued, "As you find your body relaxing, notice how your breath gets deeper and fuller. Again, presence yourself that there is nowhere to go, just everywhere to be. As your body and mind get deeper I want you to bring your attention to your thoughts. Now don't stop thinking, just don't pay attention to the contents of the thoughts or where they want to push or pull you. Notice how your thoughts will arise then fade away, into another thought, like a bubble rising to the surface of the ocean. Thoughts rise and fall, and come and go. As you are noticing your thoughts also bring your attention back to your breath and notice right before you exhale or inhale there is a moment of stillness a moment of silence, a moment of nothingness. Now that you are noticing this moment of nothingness in your breathing, bring that same level of attention to your thoughts. Notice the space before or after a thought arises. When you notice it, welcome it because that's the real you; that place beyond identification, beyond labels, which can only be described as 'I am', the feeling of pure existence before identification with thought. The more and more you can identify the gaps between your thoughts, the greater the opportunity to exercise free will and choose how to think or react. To choose a life by conscious design begins with that space between your thoughts, to change it from automatic to conscious. To begin to design a life instead of to live one by default!"

"Now once again Adam, pay attention to the trail of your breath, become aware of what it's like to have a body and when you are ready slowly open your eyes."

"Wow Tavaar that was amazing."

"Adam, can you feel an ever so slightly deeper quality of mind?"

"More than slightly Tavaar, I feel calm, centered and relaxed. That space between my thoughts is an amazing thing. I am something other than thinking. So who am I Tavaar?"

"We will begin to discover that tomorrow; for now get to bed and get some rest."

Chapter 19

The most dangerous weapon

Adam began to enjoy this concept of stillness and listening for the sound that was always there. He did not think it was the voice of God but he thought the old man's explanation had a certain charm. He allowed his attention to still and bring focus to his hearing, and there that sound was. A sort of static or a hum, which Adam reasoned must be the sound of his central nervous system working. And yet his metaphysical side suggested it might be the sound of the Universe, this sound that is always there. "What if it was the voice of God? I wonder what he is trying to communicate to me," mused Adam.

As Adam pondered the hum in his ears he saw Tavaar walking toward him with a slightly menacing grin on his face. The pine trees were framed magnificently behind him, each straight like a soldier swaying in the wind independently.

"Adam, stand up and face me. I am about to teach you a very valuable lesson, one that you may never forget. I want you to remember my commitment to you and who I am for you since what I am about to do to you may cause you to be a tad uncomfortable."

Adam cringed as the older man said this because he knew a 'tad' in Tavaar's world could be the equivalent of a free pass to a buffet lunch in Vegas for a bulimic. Still, Adam did what he was told and stood up and faced Tavaar. Tavaar was silhouetted against the backdrop of his cabin. Adam could even notice the grout between the logs. He guessed that the stillness exercise was actually beginning to slow down his mind and he was experiencing a greater level of the vividness of life. 'Wow,' he thought to himself, 'I am beginning to get it!' As Adam smirked with self–gratification, acknowledging to himself what he was learning and letting his pleasure dance across his face. Tavaar put one hand behind his back, dug for something and brought his hand to the front. While the other hand raised to meet it, Tavaar dropped his knees slightly and pointed something at Adam.

Adam's grin of self-satisfaction slipped into an 'O' of amazement and fear. Everything disappeared in the background as his mind focused on the gun Tavaar was holding in his hands and now pointing at Adam. "Is, is that loaded?" stammered Adam.

"Of course! Of what use is an unloaded gun? It's like drinking near beer, an exercise in futility. Judging from your reaction, it seems I have your attention. Or rather, my weapon does. I know what I am doing now violates every gun safety class out there, but it is to teach you something. So, Adam, what is the greatest danger to you at this given moment?"

Adam had never been on the business side of a gun before much less ever shot one. He saw what a gun could do on television and knew from the media how dangerous they were. He was amazed at how that weapon dominated his attention. He could see the barrel and the bore of the weapon, the black handle and the severe lines of the gun. This close to his face and with such focused attention, it was amazingly simple what the gun was built to do. It was completely flat, black and emotionless. What he could not get over was the emptiness and the size of the black hole in the barrel. He thought to himself,

"So this is the time of my death?" Guns, especially when pointed at you, tend to concentrate the mind on one's mortality.

"Adam, what is the greatest danger to you at this given moment?"

"The freakin' gun. What do you think?"

"Now come on, Adam, calm down. I need you to think. What is going to kill you?"

"What? You are going to kill me! Come on, I am trying to do my best with all these wacky concepts you are sharing with me." Adam screeched, half kidding and half sacred at the same time. He was in the woods in the middle of nowhere and Tavaar was not exactly a normal person. If Adam had been used to guns, perhaps he would have calmed down quickly enough to realize that he believed Tavaar would not harm him, but he wasn't.

"Once again, Adam, what is going to kill you? Please don't agitate me. I do have a loaded, government-issue Colt .45 in my hands, and it ain't the kind that Billy Dee Williams drinks either!"

"Who is Billy Dee Williams?"

Tavaar was temporarily taken back, but he recovered his composure quickly. "Never mind. What is going to kill you Adam?"

"The gun."

"No. What is going to kill you, Adam?"

"I said the gun."

"Adam, if the gun was going to kill you, I would have to come over there and beat you in the head with it."

"Alright if it's not the gun, then the bullets."

"Better answer – at least you are thinking a little, but, no. Try again Adam, what is going to be the agent of your death?"

"You."

"I'm losing my patience here, you are smarter than this. What part of me?"

"Your finger pulling the trigger?"

"Close, but still, no. What will be the actual cause of your death? What do you really have to protect yourself from?"

"You! I have already said it, damn it."

"As you can see, stress is a great teaching tool! But what part of me do you have to protect yourself from? What is my most dangerous weapon? It's not the gun, nor the bullets nor even my finger. What is it then?"

Adam was still confused. "I don't know. What?"

"Think, Adam. What caused me to raise the weapon at you in the first place?"

"Your intention! Or maybe you've gone off the deep end."

"Hmm. Hard to tell, is it?" Tavaar smiled. "Where does intention reside?"

"Your mind."

"That's it, Adam. That's it exactly! The thing you must protect yourself from is my mind. It is my mind that is the greatest danger to you. It is my mind that is my most dangerous weapon. My mind is the most lethal because without a gun, bullets or even a finger I can still be the agent of your death. But without a mind? I am rendered useless. I did this exercise to knock home a point with you." Tavaar holstered his weapon and walked toward Adam.

Adam's head was reeling, and he shied away from the older man's approach. "Tavaar, what the hell was this about? I don't understand what I'm supposed to learn from this other than knowing that when a gun is pointed at me, I feel very uncomfortable."

"Well, it's good that you don't understand at the moment, for I will explain it to you. What I have shown you was that the greatest threat to you was not the gun in my hand, but the mind, in between my ears. Think about it this way, Adam. A gun is just a lump of steel. It can be a weapon. It can be a paperweight, it can be a status symbol. It can even be a burden. But it is the mind, the mind which directs its outcome. More specifically, it's the intention of my mind, which is most dangerous to you. The intention is what directs attention. For example, if my intention was to kill you, my attention would have squeezed the trigger. Or more specifically, my attention would've acquired you as the target and then squeezed off a few rounds. Or, if I did not have any more bullets I would have clobbered you with the gun. Intention creates the space for attention, which creates the opportunity for action to fulfill the intention. Are you seeing this, Adam?"

"Frankly, Shane, only vaguely – I'm still shook up from this." Adam paused, looking slowly around at the trees along the ridgeline to the west to collect himself. 'Just breathe,' he thought. After a few minutes, he turned to Tavaar again. "So what you're saying is it's not the gun that kills me, but your mind?"

"Exactly! If you eliminate the mind, you eliminate the threat! Even if they have weapons pointed at you. No mind, no threat. I know you're wondering why I'm trying to explain this to you, and why I chose to do it with a gun. You see, in the days of old the most important weapon a warrior needed to retain was his mind. If a warrior's mind could not be taken then he could not be defeated. I can see in your confused face that this lesson is not percolating. In simple terms, your greatest asset, your greatest creator, your greatest wealth generator, your greatest lover, your greatest business attribute, is your mind. Can you see that now Adam? It's your mind. If your mind gets taken, you get defeated. Because if your mind gets taken your intention and your attention get taken. Remember what I said long ago – you are the sun and whatever you shall shine upon shall grow."

"Yes, I remember that."

"So the essential lesson of life is to keep your mind about you. A true warrior is always aware of where his mind is and he protects his mind at all costs and at all times, because he realizes that if his mind is taken, the next thing taken is his life. You're not a soldier, neither am I, but there is a lesson in that for us. We still have goals and outcomes that we are designing. When your mind gets taken you can no longer work towards your purpose or your goals. The mind can be taken by any number of things – your emotions, your wife, your kids, your boss, your neighbor, your dog, politics, gossip, righteousness, the fact that you're hungry, another's distractions, another's fires, busyness, worry – all taking your mind away from your purpose. The more that your mind is polluted, the less you produce what's in alignment with you. Be aware of who or what takes your mind, and why. The power of your attention is the most creative, or destructive, force in the universe. So if your mind gets taken you are useless to yourself."

Tavaar paused and waited for his words to sink in. The two men stood facing each other, but both looked away. A slight breeze stirred the trees.

"Can you see why I shared the concept of stillness with you? Can you see it is so important to allow the mud of the mind to settle? And why it is vital to straighten your hooks so nothing will bind you? Or why it is important to eliminate the messes in your life? It all comes down to the simple concept of protecting your mind to keep it attentive to what you choose to design. There is a huge distinction between a life by design and a life by default. Because if you're not attentive to what you are designing then how is it ever going to come into existence?"

"You're talking about protection, but protect my mind against what? My wife and kids? I don't understand that."

"Alright, you're listening to my words, but not their meaning. I just told you, Adam, but if you need a simple summary, then one word: distraction. Distraction is attending to something that is not what you've set your designs upon, something that's not in alignment with what you are committed to creating. When we first started you said you wanted to make more money and find more satisfaction."

"Yeah, and I still do want to make more money. But I am still confused how all these strange lessons, philosophies, principles, whatever you want to call them, which you share with me, put any more money in my wallet."

Tavaar's shoulders sagged for a moment, a note of exasperation passing across his face. He sighed. "Adam, you still have much to learn. Understand this: everything I'm sharing with you will create greater abundance in an individual if they allow it."

"How's that?"

"Making money. That's your example. Now, bring your mind back to work and let's look at how much attention you give to making money."

"Well that's what I do all day in the office, it's all about the Benjamins."

"Really, Adam? You mean to tell me every moment that you're in the office you are focused on generating money? Notice I said generating money, I did not say thinking about how much money you would like or how if you had more money things might be different, or wondering why you're not making more money. Think broader – when you're in the office generating money are you actually in the office? Or perhaps you're thinking about an old girlfriend, that touchdown you should've scored in high school or even what you are going to have for dinner. Most people are obsessed with making more money but they rarely focus their attention on generating money. They spend most of their days distracted or doing busy work. Someone once said the unfortunate thing about most people is that they major in minor things."

"That's clever. Yeah… So what you're saying is that although I am at the office working I am not necessarily giving attention to making money?"

"Knowing you, yes. If you were focusing attention on making money you would be making more money."

"So what am I really doing in the office?"

"That's a great question. Maybe we should find out."

"How would you do that if the problem is in my mind?"

"Well, another good question. On our way back to town I will give you an exercise to work on 'til we meet again."

Chapter 20

How to shoot

At the crack of dawn, Adam felt an iron finger poking him in the ribs, reminding him of an exercise long ago when Tavaar said that his finger owned him. He smiled to himself as he opened his eyes to see his teacher grinning above him.

"Yesterday you wanted to find out who you truly are and today I will show you a way to attain what it is that you want. Now mind you, I said 'a' way, not 'the' way. This is not an absolute exercise but one that may give you a few hints."

"I am looking forward to it." Adam stretched and sat up. He realized that clearing his head and meditating before going to sleep the night before left him more refreshed.

"Good, I have set up a few things behind the cabin. You'll need one of these for today's lesson, as well as this and this." Tavaar handed Adam a .45 caliber handgun with a pair of ear plugs and shooting glasses. Adam gingerly accepted the gun from Tavaar's outstretched hand, as if he were single and taking hold of his friend's child for the first time. His discomfort showed.

"Why?"

"Trust me. You know what that is? A .45 caliber 1911 automatic with 7 rounds in the clip, one in the chamber."

"It's loaded?" Adam asked, bravely sticking out his chest and covering his fear with bravado.

"Yes it is, and the safety is on. Be mindful when you are holding the weapon to keep the business end down range and don't point it at anyone, especially yourself, because it can cause, let's say, some pain if it discharged."

"I've never shot a gun before Tavaar."

The old man grinned and slapped Adam on the shoulder. "You don't say? Don't worry. I'll teach you how to shoot but that is not what you are here to learn anyway, is it? You're here to learn who you are and how to create a life that you choose, much like Brian Craig did. Once again, I want to remind you that this is a process. Do not expect overnight results but look to the principles of what I am going to show you and discover how to apply them to your business and life."

Tavaar guided Adam to the back of the cabin. There was a bench to stand behind and an open clearing.

"I am going to show you an interesting thing about shooting today, or let's say about hitting any target if you will. Adam, stay here while I walk the target out to where most people begin to learn how to shoot."

Tavaar walked out about 45 feet and placed a traditional bullseye target on a stick. He walked back to Adam's side and said, "Okay, shoot!"

"But I don't know how."

"So you need help or instruction?"

"Yes, Tavaar. I've told you these things bother me." He held up the gun, waving it without really thinking.

"Whoa! I already gave you the first lesson – keep the barrel pointed down range. I'm glad to hear you ask for help, because asking for help is a key principle in getting what you want in business and your life! Asking! When you ask for help you are increasing the probability of getting what you want faster than having to figure it out by yourself. But let's see why that is. So aim at that target downfield and shoot. Let's see what the results are first without instruction."

Adam dropped the clip. His hand jerked and he closed his eyes from the sparks and flame. As he squeezed the trigger and felt the recoil each time, his discomfort only grew. He hit the target once out of 15 rounds.

Tavaar then reviewed the basics of shooting with Adam. He taught him about shooting from his center line, both hands on the weapon, relaxing and gently squeezing the trigger. Adam listened, and Tavaar handed him another 15 round clip.

"Go head and shoot some more."

The second time Adam hit the target 5 out of 15 tries. He felt a little more confident but was still not comfortable with shooting.

"That's better, but your fear is still a distraction. Now I want you to pay attention Adam. Notice that your aim has improved because you are hitting the target, and that's because you've had some instruction. Now let me show you the way to guarantee your success. This is where most people fail. Most do not do this step, most just start shooting, get disappointed and never shoot again."

Tavaar reached out and turned on the safety, then went out to the target and brought it back, planting the stick in the ground about one foot away from Adam's weapon.

"What, are you serious? I can't miss it if it is right in front of me, Tavaar. Even as uncomfortable as I still feel with the thing."

"Exactly Adam, master the small first and build upon your successes. Stack the deck to win. First we start at 1 foot, then go to 2, then 3 and so on. You cannot move the target back, even an inch, unless you hit it all 15 times. Allow the target to hone you but take it one step at a time. Let me repeat something: the true purpose of a target is not to hit it, but to hone the shooter. Each time you take a shot you are getting feedback. You are practicing. If you take this exercise on as a practice in shooting, you will have no choice but to improve. The fundamental key, of course, is having a target. Without the target you would have nothing to shoot at and with nothing to shoot at, it's a waste of bullets, and a waste of time."

"Take this on as a practice in shooting," Adam Asked, "Why do I call it a practice?"

Tavaar looked at Adam closely, and spoke with quiet approval. "You know, you can be extremely attentive when you want to be. I did say a practice. Imagine if you embraced every day of your business career as a practice, a practice to make you better. Most people do things to get things done; they don't treat them as a practice. Constant and never ending practice, Adam, is the key to success."

Chapter 21

You do not get to Disney World by accident

"Adam, remember what I said about the shooting exercise the other day?"

"Yeah, I remember. You know, I think I'm getting pretty good. It's a lot more fun than I ever would have thought."

"Indeed you are. The root of excellence is practice, and I've seen you begin to excel at the practice."

"Thanks."

"I bring it up because I want to re-emphasize the power of the target. It is the target that allows you to practice hitting it. At the expense of sounding redundant, I want to say again that if you do not have a target you have nothing to shoot at so you cannot hone your aim."

"Okay. I got that. Having targets gives me something to shoot at."

"The funny thing about a target is that it is most valuable when you miss it."

"Huh?"

"Well, when you miss the target it requires you to readjust your aim. You take the feedback in and get a little better. One of the reasons why you move a target continually back is that it becomes more and more challenging. The more challenging anything is the more you pay attention to it. The more attention you give to it the better your performance becomes. Remember, 'you are the sun…"

Adam completed the sentence, "and whatever I shall shine upon shall grow."

"Yes," Tavaar replied with a smile, "and now I have another of what you call my philosophical statements to add to your notebook, which will only enhance your shooting. 'Be committed to the outcome but unattached to the result.' Did you get that? 'Be committed to the outcome but unattached to the result.'"

"Yeah, I got it, but what's it mean?"

"Think about shooting. Each time you squeeze that trigger, you are committed to hitting the target, right?"

"Right."

"Unfortunately, the catch is that often you are attached to the result. You make hitting or missing the target mean something, so when you miss it, it usually means something negative about you. This is true for everybody. But imagine if after every shot you missed you threw a temper tantrum. After your temper tantrum, do you think you would shoot better or worse?"

"Worse."

"Good. Why?"

"Because my mind would be cluttered with my anger and emotions."

"All of this is coming together for you, I see. The mud of the mind would be stirred up if you will. So to become a better shooter you need to be committed to the outcome of hitting the target but unattached to whether or not you actually do, because attachment hinders ability. I think you see the importance of a target, but let me translate it into everyday terms to show you how much design is around us, because design is what makes things happen. Fundamentally, design is the result of attention."

"I can get that," nodded Adam.

"So where was the last place you went on vacation?"

"Disney World." Adam stated, "you know, the kids and all." He smiled, a bit ruefully, but in fact he had enjoyed the trip quite a bit.

"So you took the kids to Disney World?"

"Yes."

"Bear with me then. I am going to assume something, that one day while you were driving back from the grocery store you did not take a detour to the airport, randomly jump on a plane, travel thousands of miles. Get off in another state, jump in a cab and say 'take me somewhere', and miracle of miracles you ended up in Disney World?"

"You're incredibly perceptive," Adam said with a grin. "That's not how it happened."

"That's what they pay me for, my boy. I know it did not happen that way because vacations do not happen randomly. There is a possibility that if you did one day just bring the family to an airport, you would get to Orlando, and get to Disney World instead of Sea World. Yes, a possibility of that, but the probability hovers right near zero. Just like there is a possibility that a meteor the size of Texas will crash into the planet tomorrow extinguishing the human race but the probability of that is almost absolute zero."

"Tavaar, I would never randomly travel with the kids, especially given their ages."

"I know. You're a good man, and you care about your family. But look at how the target of Disney World creates the many roads of fulfillment for it. The target creates the opportunities to hit it. Think back when you and Evelyn chose to go to Disney. Once the choice was made many other choices were then created for you to choose from. Or in simple English: You had to choose how you would get there: plane, train, car, hike. You also had to coordinate when you would go. Where you would stay. How long you would stay etc. It happened by design. Without the design, then no vacation. Without the target of Disney World, nothing else happens. Without the commitment to go, you stay at home for the week, and we both know a week's vacation at the house is not really a vacation. It's a 'honey, do this' list bonanza."

Chapter 22

Commitment is freedom

"So, Adam, are you ready to discover who you are?"

Adam lifted his eyebrows and grinned, saying with mock disbelief, "You mean I am not that sound of silence between my thoughts?"

"You think that's funny, but yes and no. You see, so many people attach themselves to their so-called Identity. They think they really know who they are. My point is that you really do not know who you are and even if you do claim to know, that individual happened by default. The funny thing is that what people really cling to as an identity is their past. Merely memories."

"You mean to tell me that what I remember to be me is not really me? All those years playing football? My first girlfriend? You mean to tell me that they are not real?"

"It's more difficult than that, Adam. Technically they are real, of course – they happened, although almost never exactly as you remember them. In that sense, they are merely things that you remember. This is scary for some people, I suppose, but you compress all that you remembered and filter it through the filters that you believe are important, all in order to support the self-created illusion of yourself."

"What? A self-created illusion?"

"Yes, the illusion of yourself. People walk around living within a concept of themselves. In a jury trial what is often the least credible piece of evidence?"

"I don't know, I've never had jury duty."

"Fair enough, but you watch television, and it's littered with cop and lawyer shows these days. If you aren't tripping over a 'remake your home or waist or face' show, you're likely watching one or another of those shows. The least credible is often an eye-witness account because you can have four people watch the same crime and all four will come up with dissimilar stories."

Adam nodded. "That's right, they always want hard indisputable evidence like those carbon fibers or pubic hairs."

"Interesting reference," said Tavaar drily, "but yes, you are right. People's memory fails them, and people remember the same things differently. To put it bluntly, whatever you remember that has made you who you are today probably did not happen that way. It is an interpretive story, not the facts if you will."

Adam sighed in disbelief. This had been a brutal trip for him, yet it was somewhat exhilarating. He was beginning to realize that there was truth in what Tavaar was saying, that he was not who he had always assumed himself to be. Even his most cherished memories were not fact, but memory, and memory was faulty, unreliable, merely an interpretation of reality.

"So Shane if I am not my memories or my thoughts or even feelings, then who am I?"

"Here is the beauty of it, Adam. You are who you choose to be. Who you freely choose."

"What is that supposed to mean?"

"Remember the thing we said about targets? The purpose of a target is not to hit it but to hone you?"

"Yes, of course."

"But having a target allows you to reach a level of fulfillment. You do not arrive in Disney World by accident."

"Sure, the probability of landing in mouse land with a hotel room and rental car is almost absolute zero unless you plan ahead."

"So who you are is defined by your commitments or your targets. Once you are committed to hitting your target and you are willing to do whatever it takes to hit the target you are then free to hit it. The beautiful thing about having a target is that it also makes it abundantly clear what you should not be shooting at! It is your commitments that set you free and your choices that enslave you. When you are committed to being healthy you know exactly what to order from the menu. When you are committed to Evelyn you know exactly who you date – only Evelyn. When you are committed to being wealthy the path unfolds before you. Commitments are freedom, Adam. Isn't it beautiful?" Tavaar smiled.

"I'm not sure I understand. Commitments can be pretty heavy. I've got a single friend who likes to say that marriage is a fine institution, but who wants to live in an institution. You know, there are times when that commitment becomes a ball and chain. You have to come home at night. You have to have sex only with her. Commitment is heavy."

"Yes, you could look at it that way, but I don't think you really do. Adam, what if commitment *is* freedom. Look at what your marriage has freed you up to do. Raise kids, build your business, experience the power of partnership. Men, and some women, forget too soon that when they were single their major and sometimes only concern was to be in a relationship. You spend most of your time and attention trying to get in a relationship or out of a relationship. And as you were gallivanting around, look at how your business fared."

"Yeah that's right. My business didn't really take off until I married Evelyn."

"Most times, people call it settling down. I say you got focused! You eliminated one of the major distractions in life, trying to find a relationship."

"So in your words, Shane, I created space for myself to expand into because of my commitment to being married. It created space for my business to be successful?"

"Very astute, Adam."

"Thanks."

"So who you are is who you commit to be."

"So I can commit to be anyone I like?"

"Yes, within reason. Some people would say that you simply are who you are; others think that who you are is the sum of what's come before. But the truth is that at any moment you can recreate yourself to be more in alignment with what you choose to create. You take what you have, what you've done and who you've been, achieve some clarity about it and think freely about where to head from there. The past and the present, it's all a form of enslavement until you allow yourself the ability to recreate. Thinking that the past traps you in a particular identity and is simply wrong-headed. Re-interpret the past, re-think your identity."

"You're getting a little 'woo–woo' with the language there, Tavaar."

"I don't think so. It all comes down to this, Adam: what are you choosing to give your attention to? For you are the sun and whatever you shall shine upon shall grow. I'll keep saying that until you know it instinctively. True freedom is choosing what you are committed to creating. Many times people tell me they just want to be free to do what they want, when they want."

"Yeah, that's what I want."

"You know what that means? Think about it. It's not what you want. What you are really saying is that you want to be a slave to your whims, fancies and passing desires! You know, Adam, nothing of value has ever been created on a whim! All things of value have originated in commitment. So what are your commitments Adam? Who are you committed to becoming? Free yourself from the chains of memory and the expectations of society."

Chapter 23

The End

"Adam, we have come to a major milestone in your journey to create a life and business by design. Now it is up to you to put all of these principles to work in your life and business. I have taught you much and you have been very committed, but today is our last meeting for some time. At the end of this meeting I am going to share a poem with you that will help guide you until we meet again."

"Have I done something wrong Tavaar?"

"No, you have been a fine student. So fine, in fact, that your teacher needs to go refill his cup."

"What do you mean?"

"Adam, I have emptied much of my cup into you. Now it is time for you to absorb what I have shared with you and make it your own, and it's time for me to spend time with my community, the community that calls to me. My Champion Circle."

"What is a Champion Circle?"

"It is a group of my peers – other people like me, who want our potential tapped. My Champion Circle and I are about to embark upon a worldwide adventure for self-refinement."

"Wow! Can I go with you?"

"In time, in time. You are not ready now, but I sense you soon will be."

"When will you be back Tavaar?"

"At the exact time I should to be of highest service to all."

"I don't know quite what you mean, but I'll trust you on that one. You are a good man, Tavaar."

"Thank you. So are you."

In that exchange between student and teacher, man to man, shibumi was present. It was a moment that defies description and yet it was a perfect moment of stillness and presence. It is a moment that cannot be captured in words, only experienced.

"So Adam, for your final lesson and until we meet again."

"I am ready, my friend."

"Adam, I have never been your friend nor do I ever intend to be for I care for your greatness too much. I told you this at the outset. I am a teacher."

"Thanks, grouch. But you're also an inspiration."

"Adam, does the world exist without you?"

"Of course it does."

"Right, of course it does, and you have tons of proof, right? You can go to the library to look at books or go to historical places for proof. There is no shortage of evidence that the world would exist without you, is there? Your friends can even tell you that if you died they would be sad but they would continue on. You have probably even been to funerals so you have seen people die."

"Yes, I have seen many people pass on."

"Once again Adam, does the world exist without you?"

"Of course it does."

"Prove it."

"Well, there are old houses and mountains over there that were here long before I was. Just look around your cabin, for instance."

"How do you know?"

"I don't know how I know. I suppose that it is what I was taught in school."

"So that was what you were taught in school? But without you, who would be taught in school? Without you, how would you know what the color red looked like? Without you what would a rooster sound like?"

"Like it has always sounded or looked."

"Again, Adam, how would you know? The painful answer is that you would not know. Fundamentally, you can never prove objectively that the world exists apart from you. Let me stretch this a bit and say that you are the world or in my language, there is no objective reality, only subjective. What is real is real because of you. Without you its reality is debatable."

"But Tavaar, that tree over there; that is real."

"Right."

Adam paused to think. "Do you see it?" he asked.

"Yes, I do."

"Then haven't you just proven to me that it exists without me?"

"Have I?"

"Yes, you have."

"No, I have not. What you heard was my voice being filtered through your brain. You are even required to listen to my language. If I were Japanese would you be able to validate what I said?"

"Hmm. This sounds like a word game more than a lesson, Tavaar."

"I don't want to get into a big philosophical debate here with you, Adam. Of course, there is an absolute reality, but we do not have the ability to see it because anything that we observe goes through our subjective lenses. The point of this conversation is to get you to confront the fact that you do create your own reality by what you give your attention to. This world is uniquely your own. If you are the creator of your world, why not create a world that works for you!"

"Right."

"Remember that the purpose of a target is to hone your aim. Your commitments and your targets create your world. Now the extreme danger is that if you are not choosing your targets, someone else is! The clearer your mind is the easier it is to hit what you are aiming for. Once you get good at hitting your target you move them. People climb mountains not because they are there but because they call forth potential. That famous line was a response to persistent questioning by reporters – why climb this mountain? Hilary just got frustrated and said 'because it's there.' That's not why he did it. He just found that he couldn't give an explanation of his motivation to those who had no understanding of his target. You continue to design your life because that is what you choose to do. It is all about choice, Adam. It is about what you choose to be committed to, because the world does not exist without you. You are the creator of your world so create one that works and find a guide when you get stuck or you want to accelerate your progress. I have been a guide for you; there will be others."

"Okay, I got it."

"Great, Adam. On that note, here is your next guide. Until we meet again."

Shane handed Adam a small scroll tied with a ribbon.

"This is a bit dramatic, don't you think, Tavaar?"

"It's captured your attention, hasn't it?"

Adam looked down and unrolled the scroll. On it was a poem:

'The bow is shattered

The arrows are all gone

At this critical moment cast aside all doubt

Shoot without the slightest delay.'

Puzzled, Adam looked up to get an explanation from his teacher who was no longer there. He looked around the bar, but the older man was gone.

Epilogue

How do I find a Shane Tavaar?

This was a question asked of me by someone who read this book as we were getting ready to publish it. I thought to myself, what a great question. This is a work of fiction but most of the book is based on events that have actually happened to me on my path of creating the life that I have, especially my company, Getting Results Coaching. Let me restate the question a different way: "How do I find a guide to bring forth more of my potential?" I would assume that is why someone would want to find a person like Shane Tavaar, who is based on a combination of many wonderful teachers and guides that I have had, with two amazing teachers at the forefront.

Finding a Shane Tavaar requires you to be very honest with yourself and to inquire within yourself to see if you are coachable. Are you willing to give up what you already know to create what you want? Because it is what you know that has prevented you from getting what you want!

It is often true that a person will not get what they want with the knowledge that they have right now; if they had the knowledge they need, they would already have what they want! To be successful you need to be real with yourself about what is missing in your life. The funny thing that I have noticed in my practice is that the more coachable you are the more money you will make in business. I have found the most successful are often the easiest to coach, especially those earning over 200k a year, while it is those that earn the least who are often the most set in their ways and confident that they "know" what they are doing. So with what they know they earn much less than they could. If you do want a Shane Tavaar or a Teacher in your world, are you willing to give up what you "know" and do different things?

It is often said that our true greatness is called forth from us by another. It is who we engage ourselves with that calls forth more of our potential. We often need to wrestle with a stranger to learn more about ourselves. It's your commitment to finding a Shane Tavaar that will bring him into existence, and if you are committed enough you will find him or her. Simply by finishing this book your mind has created the opportunity for fulfillment, of finding that person or persons to guide you to what you want to create. Perhaps my company can help you along your path but we will never know unless you reach out and make an inquiry visit us at our website www.GettingResultsCoaching.com. We have amazing coaches on staff who live the philosophy of Shane Tavaar. If you are interested in having me speak at your next engagement please visit www.KenDoyleSpeaks.com.

Ken Doyle

Founder

Getting Results Coaching

P.O. Box 218

Pinckney, MI 48169

About the Author

Ken Doyle is the top business coach and speaker. He splits the year living in Michigan and Sarasota, Florida where he spends his time boating, playing with his dogs, and enjoying life with his beautiful wife Lauren. If you are interested in finding out more information please visit www.KenDoyleSpeaks.com or www.GettingResultsCoaching.com.